Georgia

Daily Devotions For Die-Hard Kids

Bulldogs

TO PARENTS/GUARDIANS FROM THE AUTHOR

DAILY DEVOTIONS FOR DIE-HARD KIDS is an adaptation of our DAILY DEVOTIONS FOR DIE-HARD FANS series. It is suggested for children ages 6 to 12, but that guideline is, of course, flexible. Only the parents or other adults can appraise the spiritual maturity of their children.

The devotions are written with the idea that a parent or adult will join the children to act as a mentor and spiritual guide for each devotion and the discussion that may ensue. The devotions seek to engage the child by capitalizing on his or her interest in the particular collegiate team the family follows. The interest in college sports is thus an oblique and somewhat tricky way, if you will, to lead your children to reading the Bible and learning about God, Jesus, and faith.

Each devotion contains a short Bible reading (except for occasional longer stories that must be read in their entirety), a paraphrase of the pertinent scripture verse(s), a true UGA sports story, and a theological discussion that ties everything together through a common theme. The devotion concludes with a suggested activity that is based on the theme of the day. I link each day's theological message to a child's life by referring to such aspects as school, chores, video games, relations with parents and teachers, etc.

The devotions are intended to be fun for both the adult and the child, but they are also intended to be attempts to spark interest in quite serious matters of faith and living a godly life. A point of emphasis throughout the book is to impress upon the child that faith is not just for the times when the family gathers for formal worship in a particular structure, but rather is for every moment of every day wherever he or she may be.

Our children are under attack by the secular world as never before. It is a time fraught with danger for the innocence and the faith of our most precious family members. I pray that this book will provide your children with a better understanding of what it means to be a Christian. I also pray that this book will help lay the foundation for what will be a lifelong journey of faith for your children. May God bless you and your family.

ED MCMINN

Bulldogs

Daily Devotions for Die-Hard Kids: Georgia Bulldogs
© 2014 Ed McMinn; Extra Point Publishers; P.O. Box 871; Perry GA 31069

Cover design by John Powell and Slynn McMinn;
Interior design by Slynn McMinn

Every effort has been made to identify copyright holders. Any omissions are unintentional. Extra Point Publishers should be notified in writing immediately for full acknowledgement in future editions.

DAILY DEVOTIONS FOR DIE-HARD FANS

ACC
CLEMSON TIGERS
DUKE BLUE DEVILS
FSU SEMINOLES
GA. TECH YELLOW JACKETS
NORTH CAROLINA TAR HEELS
NC STATE WOLFPACK
VIRGINIA CAVALIERS
VIRGINIA TECH HOKIES

BIG 12
BAYLOR BEARS
OKLAHOMA SOONERS
OKLAHOMA STATE COWBOYS
TCU HORNED FROGS
TEXAS LONGHORNS
TEXAS TECH RED RAIDERS

BIG 10
MICHIGAN WOLVERINES
OHIO STATE BUCKEYES
PENN STATE NITTANY LIONS

SEC
ALABAMA CRIMSON TIDE
ARKANSAS RAZORBACKS
AUBURN TIGERS
MORE AUBURN TIGERS
FLORIDA GATORS
GEORGIA BULLDOGS
MORE GEORGIA BULLDOGS
KENTUCKY WILDCATS
LSU TIGERS
MISSISSIPPI STATE BULLDOGS
MISSOURI TIGERS
OLE MISS REBELS
SOUTH CAROLINA GAMECOCKS
MORE S. CAROLINA GAMECOCKS
TEXAS A&M AGGIES
TENNESSEE VOLUNTEERS

NASCAR

DAILY DEVOTIONS FOR DIE-HARD KIDS
ALABAMA CRIMSON TIDE; AUBURN TIGERS; GEORGIA BULLDOGS

IN THE BEGINNING

Read Genesis 1:1; 2:1-3.

In the beginning, God created the heavens and the earth.

Football at Georgia began in a really crazy way. A college teacher threw a ball onto a field and told a bunch of guys to go get it.

Way back a long time ago in the 1890s, Georgia didn't have a football team. All the school had was some college boys running around, jumping, and playing the fool with a football. They didn't even know what to do with it. They just sort of kicked it around.

But a UGA teacher had seen a real college football game at another school. He told the students about it, and they decided they wanted a team. That teacher held the first practice. He threw the football into the air and told the boys to get it. The strongest ones made the first Georgia football team.

Bulldogs

That teacher made the players run three miles and take a cold shower before breakfast each day. He used a rule book to teach himself and the players the rules of the game.

In January 1892, Georgia beat Mercer 50-0 in the first college football game ever played in the South. It was the beginning of Bulldog football.

Beginnings are important, but how we use those beginnings is even more important. You get a new beginning in your life every time the sun comes up and brings you a new day.

Have you ever thought that every morning is a gift from God? Well, it is. This present of a new day shows God's love for you. Each new day is full of promise. You can use it to make some wrong things right and to do some good.

How you use your new day is up to you. You should just make sure you walk with God all day long.

Try starting each morning by thanking God for the day and asking him to protect and lead you all day long.

A SECOND CHANCE

Read Acts 9:1-6, 13-15.

God said, "I have chosen Paul to work for me."

Mike Bobo needed a second chance.

Bobo is one of Georgia's greatest quarterbacks. In 2006, Mark Richt chose him to be the Dawgs' offensive coordinator. That means he is the coach of the Georgia offense.

He was the starting quarterback for UGA in 1996, but Georgia had a bad year. He was benched for the Auburn game.

The change in quarterbacks didn't help any. In the fourth quarter, Auburn was way ahead 28-7. Since Georgia was getting embarrassed, the coaches decided to give Bobo a second chance. They sent him back into the game.

Bobo led one of the greatest comebacks in college football history. With one second left, he threw a touchdown pass. It was the third

Bulldogs

UGA score of the quarter and tied the game!

The game went into four overtimes, and UGA won 56-49. Bobo had a spectacular game, throwing for 360 yards. "It's the best feeling I've ever had," Bobo said about his second chance and the win.

Paul was an evil man, persecuting and killing Christians, until he met Jesus. Then his life changed forever. Like Paul, you need a second chance now and then. Like taking a test over. Or getting another at-bat after you've struck out in a softball or baseball game.

Here's something really cool. With God, you always get a second chance. God will never, ever give up on you. He will always give you another chance when you do wrong. Nothing you can do will make God stop loving you.

You just have to go to him and ask for his forgiveness. Then you get a second chance. Every time.

***Think about a time you made a mistake.
If you got a second chance,
what would you do differently?***

UNBELIEVABLE!

Read Hebrews 3:12-14.

*Do not have an unbelieving heart
that turns you away from God.*

What a Bulldog did was so unbelievable that a player from the other team asked the ref if it really happened.

Defensive end David Pollack was a three-time All-America (2002-04). Twice he was the SEC Defensive Player of the Year.

But no one really knew who he was when Georgia played South Carolina in 2002. The Dawgs led 3-0 when Pollack pulled off that unbelievable play.

South Carolina tried to pass from its own end zone. The quarterback raised his arm to throw the ball just as Pollack got near him to tackle him. Somehow, the ball wound up in Pollack's arms. He had stolen the ball from the quarterback just as he tried to throw!

Bulldogs

The ref signalled for a touchdown. The surprised South Carolina quarterback turned to the ref and asked, "Are you serious?" He was very serious, even though the South Carolina player couldn't believe it.

Georgia won 13-7, thanks to David Pollack's unbelievable play.

You know, it doesn't really matter if you don't believe in some things. Like magic. Or that a horseshoe can bring you good luck if you nail it over your door.

But it matters a whole lot that you believe in Jesus as the Son of God. Some people say that Jesus was a good man and a good teacher and that's all.

They are wrong, and their unbelief is bad for them. God doesn't fool around with people who don't believe in Jesus as their Savior. He locks them out of Heaven forever.

If you believe, you'll go to Heaven one day and be happy with God and Jesus.

Talk to your parents about some things you don't believe in and some things you do believe in and why.

UNCERTAINTY

Read Psalm 18:1-2.

God is my rock and my fortress.

In one awful, painful moment, Kaylan Earls found out that she couldn't be certain anymore about gymnastics.

Earls had never been injured. Whatever it was she wanted to do with gymnastics, her body let her do it all through high school. And then she came to Georgia. Two weeks before her first season began, she snapped her Achilles tendon. It connects your heel to your calf muscles and helps push your feet forward when you take a step. Injuring it makes walking almost impossible it hurts so bad.

"I freaked out," Earls said. She had to have surgery to repair the tear. As she healed, she was uncertain about her body for the first time ever. Would it let her do all those things she had been able to do before, all the things that made one of the best gymnasts in the country and a Georgia Bulldog? Earls said she was "gun-shy" she was so uncertain.

She made it back, though. As a senior in 2014, she was All-America. The uncertainty was gone.

You've been uncertain, haven't you? What about a hard test you had coming up? Or a dance recital or play? You got nervous because you didn't know how you would do.

Life is like that. You will always be uncertain about some things. That's because you never know what will happen next. Like Kaylan Earls, who had no idea she would get injured.

So is there anything in your life that you can be certain about? Something or someone that will never let you down?

You can be certain about God. He is your rock. He is your fort. He will always be there for you, and he will never want anything but good for you. You can depend on God.

List some things you might be certain about in your life. Then talk about how maybe they could let you down.

HEAD GAMES

Read Job 28:20-28.

Respect God, which will show that you are wise.

A Bulldog football player was once so smart that he used his helmet to help Georgia win a game!

Way back in 1911, George Woodruff was the quarterback for Georgia. Late in the game against Sewanee, a thick blanket of fog started to cover the field. It was hard for the players to see. Woodruff decided to use a trick play to try and win the game.

When Woodruff dropped back to pass the ball, he took off his helmet and threw it down the field. In the fog, the confused Sewanee players chased the helmet thinking it was the ball! Woodruff then gave the ball to the half-back, who ran all the way down the field for a touchdown. Georgia went on to win 12-3.

Bulldogs

Since at the time there was no rule against what Woodruff did, that was a really smart play. His quick thinking helped the Dawgs win.

Being smart is one of God's gifts. No matter what's going on, you can always use your brain to be smart and make good decisions.

Have you noticed that you use your brain all the time every day? In every class at school, you have to use your brain so you'll be smarter.

The same thing applies to your faith in God and Jesus. When you go to church or open your Bible, you need to keep on thinking. You'll seek Jesus with everything that you have: with your heart, your soul, your body, and your mind.

There's nothing strange about using your brain to think about God. That's because God gave you your brain to begin with. That means he likes people to be smart.

So for you, loving God and trusting in Jesus is the smartest thing of all.

Open your Bible at random and read a few verses. Use your brain to figure out what they mean as best you can.

FACING THE MUSIC

Read Psalm 98:4-6.

*Shout to the Lord, burst into song,
and make music.*

The loudest bunch at a Georgia football game sits together and dresses funny. They're the University of Georgia Redcoat Band.

The band started in 1905 with only twenty members. They were all military cadets since the band was part of the university's military department. The first time the band showed up and played for a game was the 1906 base-ball game between UGA and Clemson.

The band grew slowly. In the 1920s and the 1930s, some musicians who weren't military cadets were allowed to join. This was the time the band first started making trips to football games. The band members traveled by train.

When LSU came to Athens in 1935 for the football game, the Tigers brought one of the

Bulldogs

biggest bands in the country with them. UGA folks were embarrassed at how small the Bulldog band was. They came up with a bunch of money and the band grew.

Today the Redcoat Band has more than 400 members and has won many awards. It is one of the best marching bands in the country.

Most Bulldog fans really like to hear the Redcoat Band play at a football game. They get up, sing, move around, and make noise.

If you like music, then you have music in your heart. But do you ever let that music come out in praise of God the way it comes out in praise of the Bulldogs? Do you sing in church, or do you just kind of stand there and mumble a few words? Are you embarrassed to sing?

Music and singing have almost always been a part of worshipping God. Think about this: God loves you and he always will. That should make you sing for joy, especially in church.

Sing your favorite song and your favorite church song. Remember that God likes to hear you sing praises to him.

SEEING THE VISION

Read Acts 26:1, 12-19.

Paul told the king, "I obeyed the vision that appeared from Heaven."

Others saw a gully that was too useless for anything but a firing range. Steadman Sanford saw something else. He saw one of the most beautiful football stadiums in the country.

A person with vision or having a vision sees what can be rather than what is. Steadman Sanford was like that.

A long time ago, Sanford was the head of athletics for UGA. In the middle of the campus was a hill with a gully at the bottom. The university rifle team used it for a practice range. Nobody else could figure out what to do with the space. It was useless.

Professor Sanford stood at the top of that hill in the spring of 1925 and had a vision. He told a student, "One day there will be a great and beautiful stadium on this site."

His vision came true. On that same piece of land today sits Sanford Stadium where the Georgia Bulldogs play. Year after year, it is named one of the most beautiful stadiums in the country. Just as Sanford envisioned.

A vision lays out a path for the future. That's because it takes work for any vision to come true. Like Sanford Stadium.

You probably have had some visions, too. Like the way you want your room to look. Maybe about playing high school sports. Or what you want to be when you grow up. Sometimes when you try to make your visions real, they don't turn out the way you hoped, do they?

God has a vision for your life. It takes the form of a plan he has for your future. God sees it as a time full of blessings. What you have to do is pray for God's guidance, to make God's vision your own. Then you work to let that vision for your life come true.

Think about your future. What do you see happening with God as your guide?

DAY 8

THE SNAKE PIT

Read Matthew 23:29-34.

You snakes! You group of vipers!

The most important man in the history of college tennis once put on a snake fight.

Dan Magill coached men's tennis at UGA for 34 years. He won more matches than any other coach in college tennis history.

Back in the 1930s before he started coaching, Magill had the idea of putting on a snake fight for the public. He had captured a six-foot king snake, and a friend had a five-foot rattler.

He put an ad in the newspaper about "the big snake fight." It said the fight would be at the UGA tennis courts at high noon on Saturday. The cost was only ten cents.

Around 200 people showed up and paid a dime to see the big fight! Magill built a wooden ring on the ground for the fight and gave the snakes the silly names of Rastus Rattlesnake and Casper King Snake.

When Magill blew a whistle to start the fight, the snakes didn't move. They just sat there and flicked their tongues! Magill poked Rastus, and the snake went after him, making Magill jump all the way out of the ring! The crowd cheered, happy that they got a bit of a show.

The snakes never did fight, though.

When you think about snakes, you probably don't get happy thoughts. In the Bible, snakes are used as a symbol for something or someone who is really bad.

Jesus used the word "snake" to describe the Pharisees. They were Jewish religious leaders who looked and acted nice and faithful on the outside. On the inside, though, they were mean and did not love Jesus.

Being true to your faith, being kind to others, and loving Jesus will keep Jesus from thinking that you are like a snake.

Act out what you would do if you found a snake in your room. Then act out what you would do if you found a person who didn't love Jesus in your room.

PRAYER WARRIORS

Read Luke 18:1-5.

Jesus told his disciples a story to show them they should always pray and never give up.

A Bulldog football player's prayer once got answered in a rather strange way.

The Bulldog football team of 1978 won so many games in the last quarter that they were called "The Wonderdawgs." Against Kentucky, they fell behind 16-0, but they rallied to trail only 16-14 with a few seconds left.

Kicker Rex Robinson, a two-time All-America, trotted onto the field to kick a field goal that would win the game.

Lineman Tim Morrison was on the sidelines praying for a good kick. But he was supposed to be in the game blocking! Georgia head coach Vince Dooley leaned over to him and said, "Your prayers have just been answered.

Bulldogs

Kentucky called time out!"

Because of the time out, Morrison had time to get into the game for the kick. If he hadn't, Georgia would have been one man short. The field goal probably would have been blocked.

Robinson's kick was good. UGA won 17-16.

Jesus told us that we should always pray and never give up. But what do you think is the right way to pray? Do you have to get on your knees? Can you be by yourself, or do you have to be in church? Should you pray out loud or can you whisper?

The truth is there is no right or wrong way to pray. What counts is that you pray, and that you mean it from your heart. Here's another truth: God hears every one of your prayers.

Sometimes — and we don't know why — God doesn't answer prayers right away. Sometimes God's answer is "no" because he always knows what's best for you even when you don't.

But no matter what, you keep praying.

Talk about the last time God answered one of your prayers.

FINISH THE DRILL

Read Mark 14:32-36.

Jesus prayed, "Father, not what I want but what you want."

The Dawgs had to finish what they started. They had to finish the drill. They did in 2002.

"Finish the Drill" was the motto of head coach Mark Richt's 2002 Bulldogs. For twenty years, UGA had been unable to win an SEC championship in football. They had a chance when they met Auburn that year. If they won, they would go to the SEC championship game.

So how did they play? Awful. In the first half, "We were just getting it handed to us," said star quarterback David Greene.

But they cut a 14-3 Auburn lead to 21-17 with 1:58 left on the clock. The Dawgs had one last chance to finish the drill.

On fourth down from the Auburn 15, Greene faked a pass to the right side and threw back to the left side. Michael Johnson jumped over a defender and caught the ball for a game-winning touchdown!

Georgia then beat Arkansas 30-3 for the SEC title. The Dawgs had finished the drill.

Being a champion is never easy. It's always hard. Quitting is heaps easier. The only way to be a champion is to never give up, never quit. In other words, to be a winner you must finish the drill.

Jesus knows what it takes to finish the drill. On the night when he was arrested, Jesus knew the suffering that faced him. He begged God not to make him go through with it.

In the end, though, Jesus yielded to God's will. He finished the drill.

Because Jesus wouldn't quit, you are saved. You get to finish the drill in your own life by never quitting on God and Jesus. That's the way to win; that's the way to Heaven.

Talk about something you did one time that was really hard. Did you think about quitting? Why didn't you?

TOUGH LOVE

Read Mark 10:17-22.

Jesus loved the rich man, but told him to sell everything he had.

UGA's gymnastics coach once kicked one of her best gymnasts off the squad. And saved her life.

In the fall of 1990, Bulldog freshman Kelly Macy was the national champion on the bars. When the season ended, she decided to get stronger and better by losing some weight.

So Macy pretty much quit eating. She lost so much weight that when she came back to Georgia in 1991, she was weak. She couldn't even do a handstand on the bars.

Head Coach Suzanne Yoculan knew something was very wrong. She used some tough love and told Macy she was off the team until she started eating and gained 25 pounds. The coach made Macy come to the gym every day, eat a meal of front of her, and watch the team practice. She wouldn't even let Macy move out of the athletic dorm into an apartment.

It worked. Macy gained weight and got her strength back. Her dad said that Coach Yocu-lan's tough love saved his daughter's life.

Your parents make you clean your room and go to bed even when you want to watch a TV show. Your dragon of a teacher loads you up with homework, even on the weekend.

Are these really just awful people who hate your guts? Nope. In reality, they're people who love you very much. They're practicing tough love, doing what's best for you. Just as Jesus practiced tough love on the rich man.

Jesus is tough on you, too. He expects you to do what you know is right even when you don't want to. Jesus knows what is best for you, just as your parents and teachers do.

Tough love is the deepest kind of love of all.

Think of something your parents make you do that you don't want to. Why do you think they do that?

TRICK PLAYS

Read Acts 19:11-16.

Some tricksters tried to use Jesus' name to drive out evil spirits. They wound up naked and bleeding.

The most famous trick play in Georgia football history never did work — except once.

When Alabama played Georgia in 1965, the Tide was the defending national champion. Nobody gave the Dawgs a chance. But they played hard and trailed only 17-10 with less than two minutes left. Coach Vince Dooley called for a trick play: the flea flicker.

Quarterback Kirby Moore didn't believe it. That's because it never worked in practice, no matter how many times the Bulldogs tried to run it. Moore finally said in the huddle, "All right, guys. Remember that thing we ran that never worked in practice? We're going to run it. Flea flicker!"

Bulldogs

The trick play worked perfectly this time. End Pat Hodgson ran a short way up the field, and Moore hit him with the pass. Hodgson lateraled (threw the ball backwards) to running back, Bob Taylor, who ran 73 yards for a touchdown.

The Dawgs got the two-point conversion for an 18-17 win, one of the greatest in Georgia history. Because of a trick play.

Sometimes simple tricks can be funny, but not all tricks are very nice and not all tricks are fun. Those that hurt other people or hurt their feelings are not nice tricks to play.

Some people will try to trick you by leading you away from God's word or Jesus. You have to be careful. They may try to trick you by telling you that what Jesus said isn't really true.

It's a funny thing about Jesus. His good news does sound too good to be true: Believe in him and you are saved and will go to Heaven one day. But it's true. It's no trick.

Think about a trick somebody played on you. How did it make you feel?

THE GREAT PIG CAPER

Read Genesis 9:1-3.

*I now give you everything that lives
and moves to eat.*

They stole a pig. And started a drive to the national championship.

Five senior football players on the 1980 Georgia team didn't have enough money to buy food for the big party at the end of spring practice. So they decided to steal a pig from the university hog farm and barbecue it.

They almost got away with it. But after the party, some freshman players took the pig's head and rolled it right at the feet of a kissing couple. While the girl screamed, the boy got a license plate number.

When Coach Vince Dooley found out about the pig caper, he was mad. He made the five players paint the wall around the practice field over and over again in the summer heat.

Bulldogs

The younger guys on the team saw how the seniors took responsibility for what they had done wrong. They even offered to help pay for the pig. The team learned to work together off the field, which helped them pull together on the field to win the 1980 championship.

Americans really do love food. We love to eat all sorts of different things, from hamburgers to chicken, pizza to ice cream. We even have TV channels that talk about food all the time. They show people how to make new dishes for their family to try and eat.

Food is one of God's really good ideas. Isn't it amazing to think that from one apple seed, an entire tree full of apples can grow and give you apples year after year?

God created this system that lets all living things grow and nourish one another. Your food comes from God and nowhere else. The least you can do is thank him for it.

Three questions to answer: What's your favorite food? What can you cook? Do you always thank God before you eat?

BEAUTIFUL PEOPLE

Read Matthew 23:27-28.

On the outside, you are beautiful.
On the inside, you are like a tomb,
full of rotten bones.

She was so beautiful she was on the cover of a national magazine. She was also a UGA volleyball player. And she liked germs.

In 1995, *Glamour* magazine put Nikki Nicholson on a cover and named her one of the Top 10 College Women of America. She was definitely striking, six feet tall and blond. But she was more than just a pretty young woman.

Nicholson was an All-American volleyball player at UGA. She was also a brilliant student who studied germs of all things. "I love pathogens," she said about the organisms that cause disease. What she liked about them was understanding them, so she could help people when they got sick.

Bulldogs

As for being on the cover of a magazine, Nicholson didn't take that too seriously. "If somebody's stupid enough to pay me for how I look, I'll do it," she said.

There was definitely more to Nikki Nicholson than a pretty face. Somebody who looked at her and judged her by her looks wouldn't know how talented, smart, and athletic she was. In other words, they wouldn't know anything about her at all.

Jesus warned us not to get too caught up in how somebody looks. Instead, you are to look at whether a person is pretty on the inside. Are they kind? Are they loving? Do they tell the truth? Do they love God and Jesus?

This makes up the inner beauty that Jesus wants from you. Jesus isn't interested at all in whether you have hot new shoes or a pretty haircut or straight teeth. For Jesus, it's what's inside that counts.

Think of a new friend you've made. When you met that person, did you use the way they looked or the way they acted to decide to be their friend?

THINK TOUGH

Read Philippians 4:4-9.

Don't worry about anything. Pray about everything, and the peace of God will be with you.

For Georgia to beat Florida, Aaron Murray had to be tough. He needed mental toughness, though, and not physical toughness.

Murray finished up at Georgia in 2013 as the SEC's greatest passing quarterback ever. He threw for more touchdowns and more yards than any other SEC quarterback In history.

In 2012, he struggled in the first half as the Dogs tried to upset the third-ranked Gators. He threw three interceptions.

If Georgia was going to win, Murray had to fight back from his bad start. He had to be mentally tough not to lose faith in himself and to believe he could make plays.

Coach Mike Bobo told Murray at halftime,

Bulldogs

"You're going to have to win this ballgame."

The game was put in Murray's hands in the last quarter. Georgia led only 10-9 when he threw a 45-yard touchdown pass. The Dawgs won 17-9, and Aaron Murray proved he was tough enough to come out on top when the going got tough.

Growing up is tough, isn't it? Grown-ups are always telling you what to do. People expect you to act a certain way. You always have too much homework to do. Life is confusing.

You've probably figured out that growing up doesn't always require that you be bigger and stronger than other kids. You have to be tough in your head and gentle in your heart. You keep plugging.

That's just what Jesus wants you to do. You keep your mind on Christ and pray that God will help you do what is right.

You pray, you trust, and you have a good time. You grow up with Jesus at your side.

List the hardest things about being a kid.
How can Jesus help you with them?

CHANGELESS

Read Hebrews 13:5-8.

Jesus Christ is the same yesterday and today and forever.

What kind of crazy game was this?

The ball was shaped like a watermelon! Players could barely hold it and couldn't throw it. Fans ran onto the field in the middle of the game and got in the players' way. Players had long hair to protect their heads because they didn't have any helmets to wear.

There were no scoreboards. The fields didn't have lights so the teams couldn't play after dark. The halves were as long as what the players wanted them to be. Sometimes they played until they got tired and decided to stop.

Teammates dragged the guy with the ball forward. Some players had handles sewn into their pants to make it easier to toss them down the field. One time a Georgia player hid

Bulldogs

on the sidelines in street clothes; that means he didn't have a uniform on. When the play started, he stepped onto the field and caught a pass.

What silly game was that? Believe it or not, it was college football back in the early days. The game has sure changed, hasn't it?

Just like football, the world around you is always changing. You might get a new teacher, or move to a new school. Your parents may get a new car for the family. You may even get a new brother or sister!

You change, too. Your feet get bigger so you get new shoes. You may have grown an inch or two since last summer so you need some new shirts and new jeans or skirts.

Even though lots of things change around you, there is one thing that doesn't change: Jesus. Jesus is the same all the time.

Jesus loves you always and his love for you never changes. No matter what.

***What has changed in your life recently?
Did you like it or did it scare you?***

RIGHT ON

Read 1 Peter 4:14-16.

If people make fun of you because you believe in Jesus, then you truly are blessed.

Kim Thompson was so nervous before her first high-school basketball game that her coach had to shove her out of the locker room. But it was because of her uniform.

Thompson was only the fifth freshman in Georgia history to start her first game. She lettered four years from 1993-96. She played for Georgia in the same kind of uniform that made her nervous back in high school.

Kim Thompson played basketball in a skirt. Not shorts; a skirt. Why would she do that? Because it was the right thing for her to do. Her faith enforced a dress code that prohibited women from wearing pants (Deut. 22:5).

"We have a standard with the Lord to keep,"

her mother said. So Thompson did the right thing even if it set her apart from the crowd. Even if some folks made fun of her.

And that first high-school game? She went out in her skirt and scored 32 points.

Kim Thompson can tell you that doing the right thing is sometimes really hard. But when you do, you feel good about yourself.

Maybe you found some money one time and gave it back to the owner. Or you helped your mom clean up after dinner even though you wanted to run off and play outside.

And what is the right thing when somebody asks you if you are a Christian? In this case, you can always know what is right. You are a Christian and you never deny it, no matter where you are or whom you're with.

In God's eyes you can never do wrong by doing right. For you, doing right always means standing up for Jesus.

List three things you can do at school that are the right things. Then list three things that are wrong to do at school.

BODY LANGUAGE

Read 1 Corinthians 6:19-20.

Honor God with your body.

UGA's athletic facilities are some of the most beautiful and modern in the country. Once upon a time, though, Georgia's football field and locker room were pretty awful.

Back in the early days of Georgia football, there was no training table for the whole team. The players ate anywhere and ate just about anything they pleased. As a result, they were in such bad shape that the 1900 game against Georgia Tech had to be cut short. Georgia won 12-0, but the players were so tired that they couldn't go anymore.

And can you believe this? The football players even wore the same jerseys in the games that they wore all week at practice. After a while, the uniforms weren't even the same color. They were a pretty sorry looking bunch!

Bulldogs

The team's dressing room was in a basement. And the site where they played the games was nothing but an old red dirt field.

Have you ever compared yourself to others and what they look like? Maybe you have a friend who's taller than you are. Or who has the blond hair you wish you had. You start thinking that you're a lot like that old red dirt field Georgia used to play football on.

That's the danger of comparing yourself to other people like your friends or TV or movie stars. Someone always looks the way that you wish you did. So you start feeling sad about yourself and the way you look.

But here's a truth to remember: Others wish they looked like you. Even God likes the way you look. After all, he made you that way.

And remember. You're so special to God that he lives with you as the Holy Spirit. Your body is God's home.

Look closely at yourself in the mirror.
Look for features that you like.
Then thank God for them.

NAME DROPPING

Read Exodus 3:13-15.

Moses asked God what his name was. God answered, "Tell them I AM has sent you."

Tweety Nolan. Goat Jernigan. Cow Nalley. These may sound like silly names, but they're the nicknames attached to some pretty cool Bulldog athletes.

Rufus "Cow" Nalley, for instance, invented the football huddle in 1895. Tackle Mike "Moonpie" Wilson and guard Joel "Cowboy" Parrish blocked beside each other.

Herschel Walker was called "The Goal Line Stalker." Georgia once had a lineman known as Eddie "Meat Cleaver" Weaver. George "Kid" Woodruff coached the football team for five seasons in the 1920s.

Bramwell "Bump" Gabrielsen was a great UGA swim coach. Harold "War Eagle" Ketron

Bulldogs

was one of Georgia's first great players and not an Auburn mascot. Georgia's 1932 basketball champions included Catfish Smith, Flip Costa, and Big Bill Strickland.

Nicknames are not given to people or to athletes any old way. They are often fun or funny names that say something about who that person is, on or off the field. First names can do the same thing; they can say a lot about a person to other people.

In the Bible, people's names reflect who they are too. Biblical names show us a little something about that person's personality or how he or she acts.

The same works with God's name. To know the name of God is to know how he has shown himself to us.

As for you, what do you think your name says about you to God? Remember this: Just as you know God's name, he knows yours, too.

Have an adult help you look up the meaning of your first name. Does it match who you are and what you're like?

TICK TOCK

Matthew 25:1-13.

*Stay alert. You don't know the day
or the hour that Jesus will return.*

In one of the strangest endings ever to a UGA football game, the Bulldogs helped the Auburn Tigers run out the clock.

In 1992, UGA was ranked 12th in the nation when the team played in Auburn. Quarterback Eric Zeier hit running back Garrison Hearst with a 64-yard bomb to give the Dawgs a 14-7 lead. But Auburn kicked a field goal and got the ball with 2:36 left in the game.

Auburn hurried down the field and called its last time out with the ball at the UGA 5. A run took the ball to within a foot of the goal line with 19 seconds left on the clock.

When Auburn snapped the ball, it popped up into the air. The quarterback got it and disappeared under a mass of big old pushing and shoving bodies. But he was short of the goal.

The Dawgs simply stayed on the ground and on top of the quarterback. That's because the clock was running. It ran right on down to zero before the players slowly picked themselves up. Georgia had a 14-10 win.

Even though you're a kid, the clock has a lot to do with your life. You have to be at school on time or you're headed for big trouble. Athletic events, classes, church, even birthday parties — they all start at a certain time. You probably have a bedtime on school nights.

All that time, every second of your life, is a gift from God since he's the one who dreamed up time in the first place.

So what does God consider making good use of the time he gives us? As Jesus' story tells us, it's being ready for the wonderful and glorious day when Jesus will return.

When will that be? Only time will tell.

Count to sixty but not real fast.
That's a minute. Any minute now
Jesus could come back.

BE PREPARED

Read Matthew 10:5-10, 16.

Go into the world and be as wise as snakes and as innocent as doves.

The Bulldogs once got ready for a big play against Vanderbilt by pretending to tie shoes.

In 1975, UGA was struggling against Vandy, leading only 7-3. The Bulldog coaches had prepared for the game by watching videos of how the Vanderbilt defense played. They saw that their defense liked to huddle over the ball and hold hands before each play. So the coaches prepared a very special, very funny play.

First, the Dawgs ran a play that had quarterback Ray Goff run around the end and get tackled. Sure enough, the Vanderbilt defense huddled up and held hands. Goff leaned over and pretended to tie his shoe while the ref set the ball down for the next play. The rest of the Bulldogs were all the way across the field.

44   DAY 21

Bulldogs

As the Vanderbilt defense held hands and watched, Goff suddenly picked up the ball and tossed it across the field to Gene Washington. Vandy wasn't ready, and he ran all the way for a touchdown.

It was called a shoestring play, and it worked. Georgia went on to win 47-3.

Anytime UGA plays any game, the coaches and the players spend time preparing so they can win. It's the same way for you, isn't it?

When you have a test at school, you prepare by studying. You prepare for a baseball game or a soccer game or a 4-H competition or a play at church by practicing for it.

Jesus prepared his followers, too. He knew he was going to die on the cross. He wanted them to be ready to spread the good news even after he went to Heaven.

You read the Bible and go to Sunday school and church. It's all to prepare you, for the day you finally meet Jesus face-to-face.

List the things you do to prepare for each day (like brush your teeth). Is a morning prayer on that list?

ANIMAL FARM

Read Genesis 6:13-21.

God told Noah to take two of every living thing into the ark.

He is among the best known dogs in the country. He is Uga.

Uga is so famous he has appeared in two movies. He was once on the cover of *Sports Illustrated*, which called him the best college mascot in the country. He was the first mascot to be invited to the presentation of the Heisman Trophy. He wore his own doggie tuxedo.

UGA's first mascot was not a bulldog but a goat. For a while, it was a bull terrier.

In the 1920s, a sportswriter said Georgia's team played as tough as Bulldogs. The name stuck. Over the years, some families loaned their pet bulldogs for some games.

In 1956, the athletic department advertised

Bulldogs

for a bulldog to be the mascot. A UGA law student said he had a puppy that might do the job. When Georgia football coach Wally Butts saw the puppy, he said, "Put him to work."

That was the first-ever Uga. Today, Uga IX watches all the Georgia home games from his air-conditioned fire hydrant.

We love our pets. Have you ever thought that God loves them, too? Your dog, your cat, or your fish — they praise God every day by being what God made them to be.

God showed how much he loved his animals when he told Noah to pack them into the ark. God saved all his varmints, not just some of the people. That tells you that all the creatures of this Earth are under God's care.

That also says you are not to be mean to animals. You treat them kindly, the same way God would. You take care of them the way God takes care of you.

What kinds of pets do you have?
Do you take good care of them
the way God wants you to?

SOUND OFF!

Read Revelation 5:11-13.

*I heard thousands and thousands
of angels singing.*

In one Georgia game, a cannon went off and cost the Dawgs a point.

UGA lost only one football game in 1966. In the last game of the season, the Bulldogs played Georgia Tech, which was undefeated. Tech led 7-0, but Georgia scored a touchdown to make it a 7-6 game.

Bobby Etter trotted out to kick the extra point that would tie the game. He was a senior who led the SEC in scoring that season. He had missed only two PATs his entire time at Georgia. But he was in for a loud surprise.

Some fans had brought a cannon to the UGA stadium to fire off after each touchdown. It went off just as Etter stepped forward to kick the extra point. That loud bang threw him off,

Bulldogs

and he missed. Tech still led 7-6.

Fortunately for the Dawgs, it didn't matter. They went on to whip Tech 23-14.

Next week, the awful cannon that had cost Georgia a point was wrapped in concrete and dropped into the Chattahoochee River.

You may not have ever heard a cannon go off, but you're used to a lot of noise, aren't you? Your school is noisy; football, basketball, and soccer games are noisy. Car horns blow, dogs bark, televisions shout.

You live in a noisy world. It's fun, but if you let it, all that noise with drown out the gentle voice of God in your heart. You need some quiet time every day. You can say your prayers, talk to God, and then listen for what he may have to say to you.

Much about Heaven will be strange, but one thing will make you feel right at home. As the Bible says, it's a noisy place. That's because everybody's whooping it up for God.

Get a watch to time yourself. Stay quiet and think about God for three minutes.

GO FISH

Read Mark 1:16-20.

"Follow me," Jesus said, "and you will fish for people."

Here's a lesson Jim Whatley once learned: Shooting a big old alligator between the eyes doesn't kill him.

"Big Jim" Whatley played football for Alabama, but he was the head baseball coach at Georgia for 25 years. He also coached basketball some. Whatley was such a good athlete he could kick out light bulbs in the ceiling.

Big Jim loved to fish. On one trip, he met up with a 10-foot alligator. He pumped two shots from his rifle right between the gator's eyes. He then swung the dead reptile into the trunk of his car to show to his wife.

Big Jim hollered to her to come over and see his treasure. When he popped the trunk open, a big, mean, very mad, and very much alive

Bulldogs

alligator went after him. He slammed the lid down and did a handstand on it to hold the gator down while it tore up his trunk.

Later, someone told Big Jim that shooting a gator between the eyes didn't kill it. It only stunned it for a little while.

Big Jim went fishing anytime he could, but he never liked meeting alligators. Do you like to fish? If not, what about some outdoor stuff like riding your bike or a scooter, jumping on a trampoline, or camping out?

Even if you don't like to drop a line into the water, Jesus wants you to be a boy or girl who fishes — for people. Jesus wants you to help reel people in for him. That is, you go fishing for people who have lost their way and you help pull them back to Jesus.

It sounds kind of like a joke, that idea about fishing for people. But Jesus meant it. He was so serious that the fish has become a symbol for his followers — Christians.

Draw a fish. What does it mean for someone to have a fish symbol on their car?

PLAN AHEAD

Read Psalm 33:4-11.

The plans of the Lord stand firm forever.

What in the world was Bulldog coach Mark Richt thinking? He planned for his team to get a penalty on purpose!

Two weeks before the Florida game of 2007, the head Bulldog told his players he wanted a celebration penalty after the first Georgia touchdown. He even said that if they didn't get a penalty, he would have them running at 5:45 in the morning.

So the Bulldogs did it — way bigger than the head coach expected. When running back Knowshon Moreno scored in the first quarter, all sixty Bulldog players ran onto the field! The Dogs wound up getting two penalties, not one.

Coach Richt didn't care. It was all part of his plan. He knew that the Bulldogs would be in real trouble against Florida if they didn't play with excitement. He wanted the entire team to be excited and pumped up for the rest of the game.

Coach Richt's plan worked. The excited and fired-up Bulldogs were still celebrating when the game was over. Georgia won 42-30.

People make plans every single day. You do, too. You plan to go to school. You plan to do your chores. You plan to go spend some time with your grandparents.

But what if something happens to mess up your plans? What if you wake up sick and your plan to go to school doesn't work out? Sometimes even when you make a great plan, it doesn't work out, does it?

God has plans for you, too. God's plan for you has nothing but good things like happiness, love, and kindness. But it will work only if you make him the boss of your life.

What are your plans for tomorrow?
Tomorrow night, think back and see if
they turned out the way you planned.

FRUIT TREES

Read Matthew 7:15-20.

A good tree bears good fruit, but a bad tree gives only bad fruit.

Apples and oranges go together quite nicely in UGA football history.

Georgia lost a big game to Clemson 29-0 way back in 1903. After the tough loss, Bulldog star Harold "War Eagle" Ketron made a deal with the Clemson players. If the Tigers beat UGA's rival Georgia Tech, the Georgia players would give them anything they wanted for each point scored over 29. What the Clemson players wanted was apples!

Clemson slaughtered Tech 73-0, and the UGA players made good on their deal. They delivered to Clemson forty-four bushels of red apples they paid $1 a bushel for.

Late in the 1942 Orange Bowl, the Dawgs were leading Texas Christian University 40-7.

Bulldogs

Guard Harry Kuniansky sat on the bench and began celebrating the Georgia victory early. He squeezed the juice out of a whole mess of oranges into his helmet to drink.

Suddenly, the coach yelled for Kuniansky to get back in the game. Hurrying, he jammed his helmet on without pouring the juice out. He played the rest of the game with orange juice running all down his face!

Just about everybody loves fruit and fruity desserts. What do you like? Apples, grapes, bananas, mangos? Even the fast food places have hot apple pies. A big grocery store has strange fruits you may never have heard of like kumquats. Say that really fast five times.

But have you ever seen or smelled a piece of rotten fruit? It's awful!

To God, people are like fruit trees. He wants you to produce good fruit. You do that by showing love to others just as Jesus did. You're kind and gentle, and when people see you, they smile. That's good fruit.

Draw a picture of your favorite fruit.

DAY 27

TALK THE TALK

Read Mark 16:14-16.

Jesus told the disciples, "Go every-where and preach the good news to everyone."

Frank Ros was a big tough linebacker for the Bulldogs. When he was little, though, he cried every day at school — because he couldn't talk to anybody.

Ros was the team captain for the 1980 national champions. He was born in Spain, and his family came to America when he was 6. On the ship, he heard his first words of English: "Good morning."

In Spain, Ros was so smart that he started school when he was 3 years old! In America, though, he had a big problem: He couldn't speak English. He couldn't talk to anybody!

"All the kids looked at me like I was crazy," Ros remembered. The only thing he under-

Bulldogs

stood about his new school was lunch.

It took little Frank several months to learn enough English to talk even a little bit. In the meantime, he cried all the time because he was so lonely and confused. He used sports, especially football, as a way to talk to people.

You take it for granted that when you talk to somebody at school, they will understand you. But how awful would it be if your teachers didn't understand a word you said!

Now think about this. All over the world people speak different languages; they can't talk to each other. But billions of those people from all the countries of the world are giving their lives to Jesus. They are becoming Christians. How cool is that?

You see, everybody in the world has words for hope, love, joy, and God. And Jesus speaks those words better than anybody else — no matter what language is being spoken.

Pick three foreign languages and learn the word for "hello" in them. Then at school, walk up to someone and say hello in one of them. See what happens.

NOT WHAT THEY SEEM

Read Habakkuk 1:2-4.

God, why do you put up with the wrong things people are doing?

A pile of hay once saved a game for the Georgia Bulldogs.

In 1927, the Dawgs traveled to New Haven, Conn., to play Yale University, a football power back then. UGA was a big underdog.

But, hey, these were the Dawgs. They had no intentions of losing and led 14-10 going into the last minute of the game. It looked like Yale had pulled out a miracle, though, with a last-minute touchdown pass.

Two officials signaled touchdown. Yale had won. Or so it seemed.

But wait! During the week of the game, the field had been covered with hay to protect it from a lot of rain. Before the game, the hay had been raked into piles. Those piles covered the goal line and hid it. The Georgia tackler wouldn't let the Yale player move until the refs shoved all the hay aside.

Sure enough, the Yale receiver was a yard short of the goal line. While it looked like Yale had won the game, Georgia did.

You know, sometimes things just aren't what they seem. It's like a mirror in a fun house at the fair. Have you ever seen one of those? It makes you look all wacky and distorted.

It's that way with the world; it looks all out of shape, like nobody's in charge. We have wars everywhere. People hurt and kill other people. Children go to bed hungry at night. What's going on?

That's what Habakkuk asked God long ago, and God answered him. God said things aren't what they seem. He said he was in control and one day he would make everything all right.

We just have to trust and believe in God.

As Habakkuk did, name some things you'd like to see God change about this world. Pray for those changes.

THE SCAPEGOAT

Read Leviticus 16:20-22.

*The priest puts the sins of the
people on the goat's head.*

Back before there was a bulldog named Uga
or a bulldog at all, there was a goat.

UGA's first football game was in 1892 against
Mercer (a school in Macon). The Georgia mascot for the game was a live goat. Georgia fans
laughed when a bunch of students drove him
across the field before the game.

After Georgia won the game 50-0, the fans
rode the players around on their shoulders.
Some of them even rode the goat.

Three weeks later, Georgia played its next
football game, against Auburn in Atlanta. The
goat made the trip, and he was all dressed up.
He wore a black blanket with red letters — U
and G — on each side. He also had on a hat
with red and black ribbons. The goat drew a

whole lot of applause from the Georgia crowd.

For some reason, the goat disappeared into history. Two seasons later, the UGA mascot was a solid white bull terrier that belonged to a student. Years later, Uga the English bulldog became the mascot as it is today.

The Bible speaks of a particular type of goat. It's called a scapegoat. It bears the blame for somebody else's sins or wrongdoing.

What a set-up! Don't clean up your room? It's that messy goat. Make a bad grade on a test? The goat didn't study.

With a scapegoat, you don't have to pay for your mistakes. You get off scot-free. That's exactly the way forgiveness works with Jesus.

Your sins — the things you do that God doesn't want you to — make God unhappy with you. But Jesus steps up and says, "Daddy, I'll take the blame. I'll be the scapegoat."

God lets his own son do that because he loves you so much.

Name some things your scapegoat could take the blame for. Then ask God for forgiveness for them in Jesus' name.

DAY 30

LIVE ACTION

Read James 2:14-17.

Faith without action is dead.

Missouri talked. Georgia played. Georgia won.

A Missouri player had some nasty things to say about Georgia before the Tigers' first-ever SEC game in 2012. He said he had watched the Dawgs' first game of the season and that they played old man football.

UGA head coach Mark Richt couldn't believe the player said that. Even the coach's mother didn't like it. Quarterback Aaron Murray said the insult helped fire the team up.

On Saturday, the time for talking was over; the time for playing had come. The old men from Athens went into Columbia and took everything the Tigers could throw at them.

Missouri led early in the third quarter, but the Dawgs took control of the game from then on. They outscored Missouri 32-3 the rest of the game and won going away 41-20.

In the excited Georgia dressing room after the game, Murray and a linebacker held up a sign that said "Grown Man Football." The Dogs didn't talk; they celebrated.

Talk is cheap. By itself, it just isn't worth too much. How much fun is it to sit around and listen to somebody talk? You get all squirmy because you want to get up and *do* something.

It's that way in your faith life. In church, you may like singing songs and watching baptisms. But sitting through a sermon sometimes is hard, isn't it?

Even Jesus didn't just talk. He almost never was still. He constantly moved from one place to another, healing and helping people.

Just talking about your faith doesn't really show it. You show that Jesus is alive by making your faith alive. You act. You do the kinds of things for people that Jesus did.

List some things you can do tomorrow to show that your faith is alive. Do them.

DAY 31

STRANGE BUT TRUE

Read Philippians 2:5-11.

Jesus is God, but he became a servant and died on a cross.

The Georgia-Ga. Tech football game of 1904 featured what may be the strangest play in the history of college football.

Georgia punted one time from its own end zone. Back then, the goal posts were on the goal line. When the ball was kicked, it hit the goal posts and went backwards over a high fence around the field.

The players all stood around wondering what to do. Strangely enough, the refs ruled the ball was still in play. The players began a game of king of the mountain, trying to climb that fence and get the ball. One player would get to the top and a rival would yank him back down into the mud.

Finally, a Tech player and a Bulldog made it

up and over the fence. On the other side was a bunch of high grass. The two players had to search around in the grass to find the ball while a ref watched everything they did.

Finally, the Tech player spotted the ball and fell on it. The referee signaled touchdown! It's strange but it's true.

A lot of things about life are strange. Isn't it strange that you can't eat all the sugar you want to? Isn't it strange that you can't play all the time when everybody knows that's what kids are good at?

God's kind of strange, too, isn't he? He's the ruler of all the universe; he can do anything he wants to. And so he let himself be killed by a bunch of men who nailed him to two pieces of wood. Isn't that downright weird?

And why did God do it? That's strange, too. He did it because he loves you so much. In the person of Jesus, God died so you can live, so you can be with him one day in Heaven.

List five things about God that are strange. Tell why they're strange.

GOOD SPORT

Read Titus 2:6-8.

Set an example: Do what is good.

Here's one for you. One of Georgia's greatest athletes got his nickname because one time he bit the head off a catfish!

When he was in high school, Vernon Smith won a bet against some high school buddies. He bit the head off a catfish he had caught in the Ocmulgee River.

Vernon "Catfish" Smith played football, basketball and baseball for Georgia. In 1929, he became a legend when he scored all 15 points in the 15-0 win over Yale in the first game ever played in Sanford Stadium.

He also scored the winning basket in the 1932 Southern Conference basketball tournament (back before the SEC). He then stole the ball with ten seconds left. He took off with the ball, but two players from the other team ran into him so hard that they knocked him into the stands.

Catfish was such a good sport that instead of getting mad, he picked himself up and shook the opposing team captain's hand! He didn't even shoot the free throws but let the 26-24 score stand. That's good sportsmanship!

Good sportsmanship means more than just following the rules and not cheating. It means you treat the other players with respect. You don't play dirty. You don't say ugly things to them. You don't try to hurt them.

Believe it or not, the Bible talks about good sportsmanship. It's called the Golden Rule: You treat people the way that you want to be treated by them. You act that way all the time and not just while you're playing a game.

If you follow the Golden Rule in sports, at home, at school, and in all things, then you are living the way Jesus wants you to.

What sports do you play? How do you show good sportsmanship in them? What about off the field?

THE JESUS WAY

Read Romans 13:10-12.

*Behave decently like in the day-
time, the way Jesus would.*

The most famous twins in the history of women's college basketball did things exactly the same way. Including the way they ate Fruit Loops.

Twin sisters Coco and Kelly Miller shared the court at Georgia from 1997-2001. *Sports Illustrated* pretty much called them the best twins ever to play the game.

Coco and Kelly didn't just play basketball together. They used their own language to talk to each other on the court. They wore similar clothes; they had the same smile; they looked exactly alike except for a freckle or two.

When the team ate meals together at places like IHOP, they both ordered buttermilk pancakes. They drowned them in strawberry and blueberry syrup. One Bulldog teammate said that if one twin raised her fork, the other one would, too.

Perhaps the freakiest thing they did together, though, involved Fruit Loops. Without thinking about it, each twin would always leave two loops floating in her bowl. "Man! How'd they do that?" one teammate asked.

They just did it the Miller Twin way.

Even as a young person, a kid, you have a certain way that you live. You're a Bulldog fan. Maybe you live in the country. Or in town. Do you wear jeans to school? Or shorts? You have a favorite video game and TV show.

Then there's your faith. You're a Christian. That means that as a way of life, you follow Jesus. You do your best to act and to think like Jesus would. That means you always try to act in a loving manner toward other people.

It's The Jesus Way. It should be your way all the time.

Make up a story about Jesus being at your school. Tell how you think he would act in class and in the lunchroom.

DAY 34

BIG MISTAKE

Read Mark 14:66-72.

Peter remembered Jesus had said to him, "Three times you will say you don't know me." Peter cried.

The Bulldogs got a star football player because some coaches made a mistake. They called him on the phone.

Bill Krug was a first-team All-SEC defensive back in 1976 and '77. He was part of one of the most famous plays in Bulldog history in the 1976 Florida game. The Bulldogs stopped the Gators on fourth-and-one and came from behind to win 41-27. They won the SEC.

From Maryland, Krug had pretty much decided to play for the University of Maryland. He didn't know much about UGA.

But Georgia pushed hard late. He visited Athens and liked what he saw. So Krug told coaches from both schools that he wanted a week to think about it and not to call him.

The Maryland coaches blew it. They called Krug a few days later, and that made up his mind. He was headed to Athens.

Only one man has ever walked this Earth and been perfect. That was Jesus. You're not him. That means you will make mistakes. You will not make all hundreds on your tests. You will not make every play in softball or soccer. You will trip and fall sometimes and embarrass yourself. You will be mean to others sometime.

All your mistakes can be forgiven if you ask God for forgiveness. That means God forgets about them. Even Peter's awful mistake in denying that he knew Jesus was forgiven because he came back to Jesus. He went on to be the main man in starting the Christian church.

The one mistake you must never make is to kick Jesus out of your life completely. God won't forget about that one.

What mistakes did you make today that hurt other people? Ask God for forgiveness of them.

I DIDN'T KNOW THAT!

Read John 8:31-34.

You will know the truth, and the truth will set you free.

Prayers he didn't even know about changed Alec Millen's life.

Millen had a good life in Athens. He was a third-team All-American lineman for the Dogs in 1992. He had lots of friends; he knew a lot of girls. But something was wrong inside, in his heart; he just didn't know what.

He had been raised in a Christian home, and he went to church in Athens. But he felt his faith was empty. He didn't really live for Jesus.

All the while a teammate was praying for him every day. For more than a year, without telling Millen, that unknown football player prayed for his teammate to be saved.

In May of 1991, Millen went with some other players to a revival service. A man there told about his faith in Jesus. That night, Millen gave his life to Jesus. Those prayers had been answered. He eventually went into seminary and into the foreign mission field with his wife.

Alec Millen's life was changed in large part by prayers he knew nothing about.

When you don't know something, it's called ignorance. It doesn't mean you're a dumb bunny; you just don't know it.

That's why you go to school. To learn things. There's a whole lot you don't know. Like how they get toothpaste into the tube. How they make paper from trees. How birds can sing.

You get along all right without knowing all that stuff, don't you? But it makes a big difference if you don't know about Jesus. In that case, ignorance sets you apart from God. So you read this book and you read the Bible and you go to Sunday school to help you learn about God and Jesus.

And that's worth knowing about!

Explain how not knowing Jesus is really a bad thing for you.

DAY 36

WATER POWER

Read Acts 10:44-48.

Peter asked, "Can anyone keep these people from being baptized with water?"

Talk about rude! Bulldog fans once had the water hoses turned on them after a game.

In November 1986, UGA went into Auburn and upset the 8th-ranked Tigers 20-16. With 54 seconds left, Georgia got an interception to wrap up the big win.

Not surprisingly, happy Bulldog fans by the bunches ran onto the field. They got a little out of hand, though, when they started tearing up the turf to take home for souvenirs.

Needless to say, the Auburn folks weren't very happy about their grass being ripped up. But they really got upset when those Bulldogs decided they should pull down a goal post to celebrate the win.

Bulldogs

Auburn's security people decided they had to do something to protect the goal posts. So they pulled out what they called their "water cannons" and turned the water on. The totally soaked fans ran from the field to escape the stream of water.

Ever since, the game has been called, "The Battle Between the Hoses." That's a joke on Georgia's home games, which are always said to be played Between the Hedges.

Do you like to go swimming? Or take a boat ride? Man, the beach is fun with all that sand, sun, and water. Is anything more exciting than a water slide?

Water is fun, but you need it to stay alive, drinking it every day.

Water is even a part of your faith in Jesus. It's called baptism. A person who is baptized — including you — is marked by the water as belonging to Jesus. It tells the world you are a Christian and that Jesus is your Lord.

Have you been baptized? If so, talk about what it was like. If not, is it time?

GOOD NEWS

Read Matthew 28:1-10.

The angel said, "Jesus has risen, just as he said he would! Take a look at where he was buried."

Ty Frix was confused. He couldn't find his locker. He didn't know it was because he had some good news waiting for him.

Frix walked on to the Georgia football team in 2008. He was given a jersey that, he said, didn't have a real number on it. His number was 132! He was trying to be the long snapper for the Dawgs, the player who centers the ball on punts, field goals, and extra points.

Before the 2009 season, Blair Walsh, the UGA placekicker, told Frix to meet him in the locker room to practice kicks. But when Frix got there, he couldn't find his locker. Somebody had taken his name off it. That's when a smiling Walsh took him into the "real" locker room, the one for the players on the team. There was a locker with Frix's name on it. He now had a real number, and he was the long snapper for the team. He was a Bulldog!

For Ty Frix, that was really good news.

It's lots of fun to get good news. Like when your teacher tells you that you made a good grade on a test. Or when your parents tell you that you're going to the beach.

People, especially grown-ups, get news all the time. Some of it's good; some of it's not. You've probably seen your mom or dad watching a news channel on TV.

News is about what's happening right now. That's why it's news. But here's something really strange. The biggest news story in the history of the world is almost two thousand years old!

The greatest and the best news story of all time happened the morning Jesus rose from the dead and walked out of his tomb.

Write a news story about something in the Bible. Read it to your parents.

DAY 38

FIRE IN YOUR HEART

Read Romans 12:9-16.

*Never let the fire in your heart
that burns for Jesus go out.*

The Bulldogs once were so fired up and excited that they threw a dogpile so big a 330-lb.
lineman couldn't breathe!

The Bulldogs of 2007 finished ranked No. 2
in the country. The Alabama game that year
went into overtime, and the Tide kicked a field
goal for a 23-20 lead. The Dawgs decided to
try to win it on the first play with a touchdown.

Quarterback Matthew Stafford threw a perfect pass to Mikey Henderson in the end zone.
With one play, Georgia had a 26-23 win.

Like their fans, the players went wild in celebration. 330-lb. lineman Chester Adams, nick-
named "Cheese," lumbered onto the field and
flattened Henderson with a wrestling move.
That started the dogpile as the rest of the

Bulldogs

happy Bulldogs dived on. Henderson said he heard Cheese say that he couldn't breathe at the bottom of that dogpile.

The Dogs went crazy after the win over Alabama because they were so excited that they couldn't help themselves. What makes you act that way, like you have a fire in your heart so you want to jump around like you have ants in your pants?

You probably don't get too excited in church, do you? Maybe you mumble the words to the songs. Or you sit there and look like you're at the dentist's office.

But God calls you to love him like you have a fire in your heart or ants in your pants. You worship God because you love him. You love God because you can't help yourself.

Worshiping God is not some awful chore you have to endure. It should be one of the most joyous and exciting things you do.

Draw a picture of you with ants in your pants. Do you get that excited about going to church?

DAY 39

NO JOKE!

Read Mark 12:28-31.

Love God with all your heart, all your soul, all your mind, and all your strength.

No joke. Vince Dooley coached some of the greatest athletes in college football history, including Herschel Walker. And he said the most incredible player he ever had was a walk-on who appeared in one game.

That player was Mike Steele who walked on and never missed a day of practice in five seasons. He played a little in the 44-0 romp over Tennessee in 1981; that was it.

Even at Georgia, Steele wanted to be a soldier. He once rappelled off the bridge at the stadium and was arrested by campus police. After he left Athens, Steele was a leader in the *Black Hawk Down* incident in Somalia. A hit movie was made about it. He received a

Bronze Star for his bravery.

He was wounded and was given up for dead in the hospital. No joke: He got out of his hospital bed, went down the hall, and climbed on a treadmill. The exercise drove the blood clots that had been killing him out of his lungs.

Dawg guard Tim Crowe echoed what Coach Dooley said about Steele: "He is my hero."

Good jokes can make us laugh, but the Bible doesn't have a whole lot of them, does it? That's because the good news of Jesus and salvation is something that we all should take very seriously.

While Christians don't laugh at Jesus, many of them treat what he taught as if it were a joke. They may say they love God, but they hate people of a different skin color or who speak a different language. They claim to love God, but are mean to other people at school.

Jesus wasn't joking when he said you show how much you love God by the way you act.

Tell your favorite joke. In Heaven with Jesus, you will laugh all the time.

BONE TIRED

Read Matthew 11:27-30.

Jesus said, "Come to me and I will give you rest."

Coach Mark Richt was tired to the bone, but he couldn't let the Georgia people down.

After the Dawgs won the SEC championship in 2002, Richt had to speak to a lot of people night after night. He loved doing it, but it just wore him down and got him tired.

One evening, after he spoke at a church, he finally realized how tired he was. He decided not to spend his usual hour signing autographs and left the church.

At a traffic light, a little boy with a Dawg cap on asked him for a signature. Richt rolled down the window and signed the boy's cap. He then told his driver to turn around. It didn't matter how tired he was. He wasn't acting like a Georgia Bulldog, he told himself. No matter

Bulldogs

how tired he gets, a Bulldog always finishes what he starts in winning fashion.

Back at the church, people were on their way home. He was too late. But Coach Richt knew he had to make things right. He was bone tired, but he arranged to come back the next day and sign autographs just as long as the excited fans wanted him to.

Don't you just get tired sometime? Maybe after a tough day at school when you stayed up too late the night before. Have you ever gotten so tired on a trip that you fell asleep in the back seat of the car?

Everybody gets tired, especially grown-ups. And sometimes, like grown-ups, you have to do what Coach Mark Richt had to do. You have to finish no matter how tired you are.

When you're tired and just worn out — that's a good time to stop a minute and pray. When you do that, you have the power of almighty God to help you and give you strength.

Talk about the last time you fell asleep on the floor. Why were you so tired? Did you know God can give you energy?

GREAT EXPECTATIONS

Read John 1:43-49.

Nathanael asked, "Nazareth! Can anything good come from there?"

The winningest coach in UGA football history wasn't what anybody expected.

Georgia football was in a big mess in 1963. The fans wanted a "name" head coach. They wanted somebody famous, a proven winner.

Instead, the athletic director hired a coach whom nobody had ever heard of. He had never even been a head coach. In fact, when the school president introduced him at a press conference, he forgot his name! A lot of folks grumbled about this new coach.

Then came his first game, against Alabama. The Tide crushed the Dawgs 31-3. The next week some folks said, "What did you expect?"

Bulldogs fans didn't expect what they got: the school's greatest football coach ever. He won 201 games, six SEC titles, and the 1980 national championship. He was the SEC Coach of the Year seven times and the national Coach of the Year twice. In 1994, he was inducted into the College Football Hall of Fame.

He was Coach Vince Dooley.

Everybody expects a lot of stuff from you, don't they? Your parents expect you to mind your manners and behave. They expect you to do your chores, like keep your room clean. They expect you to make good grades.

Your teachers expect you to sit down and be quiet in class. They expect you to do all your class work and your homework.

Have you ever thought that God expects a lot from you, too? Nathanael didn't expect anything good to come from Nazareth, but it did. And God expects something good to come from you, too.

What God expects from you — to live like Jesus — is more important than anything else.

**Name some things God expects from you.
How are you doing?**

YOU NEVER KNOW

Read Exodus 3:7-12.

Moses asked God, "Who am I to go before Pharaoh?" God answered, "I will be with you."

John Jenkins is a really big man. You won't believe what sport he liked while he was growing up.

Jenkins played nose tackle for Georgia in 2011 and 2012. At 6-foot-3 and 351 pounds, he was a big, big Bulldog.

He grew up big. His mother had to tell him not to drop into a chair or he would break the springs. He once crashed his mother's bed just by sitting on it! When he visited other homes, he sometimes stood up rather than take a chance on busting the chairs.

He played football and basketball, but they weren't the sport he was the best at. That was — here it comes: Bike racing! "That's for real,"

Bulldogs

his mother said. He was by far the biggest kid on the track, and some of the other riders were a little scared about racing him.

Was he any good? Jenkins claimed he was better at bike racing than he was at football and basketball. And he was good enough at football to be second-team All-SEC.

You're like big John Jenkins and Moses. You never know what you can do until you try. You may think you can't play football, cook supper, or run the lawn mower. But have you tried?

Your parents sometimes tell you to do things you think you can't do. God is the same way. You just never know what God is going to ask you to do. Sing a solo in church. Tell someone else about Jesus. Help an old person.

You may think, "I can't do that." But if it's something God wants you to do, you can. You just have to trust him. With God's help, you can do it.

Think of something you've never tried before but would like to do. Decide to do it and pray for God to help you.

THE INTERVIEW

Read Romans 14:9-12.

We will all have to explain to God everything we have done.

Meghan Boenig nearly blew her job interview at UGA before she ever said a word!

When a grown-up wants a job at Georgia, he or she must have an interview. She answers questions from the people who will hire her so they will know something about her.

Boenig is the coach of the women's equestrian or horseback riding team at Georgia. She is one of the most successful coaches in UGA history. In 2014, the Dawgs won their sixth national championship. Entering the season, their record at home was an incredible 50-3.

But she had to have a job interview first. It was in 2001, and the UGA equestrian program didn't even exist. She would be the first coach ever if she got the job.

Bulldogs

So what did she do wrong? She showed up for her interview wearing a shirt that definitely had an orange tint to it. Orange — as in UGA's big rivals like Florida, Tennessee, and Auburn. "It was much more pink," she said.

But Boenig knew she had made a mistake. When she was called back for a second interview, she wore red. And she got the job.

You've probably never had a job interview, but you will one day. You may have an interview to get into some school club or group.

Interviews are hard because people ask you questions and judge you. That means they decide whether you are good enough for what they want. Nobody likes to be judged.

One day, you will show up in Heaven. The Bible tells us that we all will be judged by God. You will have an interview with God.

Talk about being nervous! How in the world can you be good enough for God? All it takes is Jesus. Jesus makes you good enough.

Pretend you're being interviewed by God. What would you tell him about yourself?

SIGHT UNSEEN

Read 2 Corinthians 5:6-10.

We live by faith, not by sight.

An injured Bulldog star standing on the sideline saw something nobody else did. The result led to a game-winning touchdown.

Chip Wisdom was an All-SEC linebacker in 1971. The season ended that year on national TV on Thanksgiving night against Georgia Tech. The Dawgs were ranked seventh in the nation with one loss, but they were in deep trouble. With only 28 seconds left, they trailed 24-21.

UGA called time out to call a play. A knee injury had kept Wisdom out of the game, so he was standing there when the coaches and the quarterback decided on a play. They chose a pass play with senior flanker Jimmy Shirer catching the ball. The team huddled up.

To his surprise, Wisdom saw Shirer standing next to him. He hadn't heard the play call and wasn't in the game! Wisdom grabbed him, told him what play to run, and sent him into the game.

Shirer caught a pass to the Tech 1. Georgia scored with 14 seconds left for a 28-24 win.

"Seeing is believing" is an old saying that means if you can't see it then you don't believe it. Thomas, one of Jesus' disciples, said he would not believe that Jesus was alive after his crucifixion until he saw him.

But eyesight is about the physical world, the world around us that God created. Christians believe also in a spiritual world. It's the world in which God, Jesus, and the angels live. It's a world you can't see with your eyes.

But you know God, you know Jesus, you know God is in control. That's because as a child of God, you live by faith and not by sight.

You believe, so you see. Not with your eyes but with your heart and your soul.

Close your eyes. What can you see? Call out the things you believe are around you. This is the way faith works.

DAY 45

SMILING FACES

Read Isaiah 35:5-10.

*Those who find Jesus will also
find joy that lasts forever.*

Many of his UGA teammates were scared to death of DeAngelo Tyson.

Tyson played in fifty games for the Bulldogs from 2008-11, starting as a junior and a senior on defense. In 2011, he won a coaches' leadership award and played in an all-star game.

Center Ben Jones said Tyson "was a little scary. I was wondering if he wanted to kill me every day." He was certainly big enough to do some damage at 6-foot-2 and 306 lbs.

Tyson was scary for a reason other than his size. He didn't smile. Ever. His face relaxed into a frown, and he was so calm and mild-mannered that he rarely changed expression.

But when Jones and his fellow Dawgs got to know Tyson, they found one of their favorite people. "He's a great guy," said receiver Tavarres King. But "I can't remember the last time I saw him smile."

Tyson's roommate, tackle Cordy Glenn, said he saw Tyson smile more than once when he got done with workouts. "I'm not the type of guy to smile all the time," Tyson said.

A smile is a wonderful thing. When you smile at someone, it makes them want to smile back at you. That's the way a smile works. It seems to make everybody around you happy, like turning on a bright light in a dark room.

And, hey, you have a good reason to walk around with a goofy smile on your face all the time. Not because of a joke you've heard or from anything you've done but because of what God has done for you. God loves you so much that he gave you Jesus so you could live with him in Heaven one day.

Now that's something to smile about!

Stand in front of a mirror and make some different smiles. How did you feel? How does your smile make others feel?

GOOD DOG!

Read Psalm 139:1-6, 13-14.

*I praise God because of the
wonderful way you made me.*

The Dawgs were big underdogs when they played LSU in 1978, but they had Uga III on their side.

The LSU mascot is a big, ferocious live tiger named Mike. Before each game, a truck pulls Mike's cage around the field. When the truck stops, Mike roars into a microphone, and the LSU crowd goes nuts.

On that night, little Uga III stood right in the middle of the field in the tiger's way and wouldn't move! The big cat let loose with a mighty roar. Uga didn't even blink. That really made Mike mad. He stood up on his hind legs, rattled his cage, and let loose with his loudest, scariest roar.

A fascinated UGA head coach Vince Dooley

Bulldogs

was watching the whole encounter. After Mike roared a second time, Uga took a couple of steps forward and barked. Mike ran to the back of his cage in fear.

An excited Coach Dooley told his players he had seen Uga face down a Bengal tiger. "We got 'em tonight," he said. He was right. The Dawgs won 24-17.

We respect and admire animals such as Uga. Isn't it fun on a trip to spot wild turkeys, foxes, or deer in the woods? And a zoo is one of the most fun places in the world to visit. Who in the world could dream up a walrus, a moose, a tiger, or a bulldog?

Well, God dreamed them all up, just like he did the possum and the rattlesnake. And just like he dreamed up you.

You are special. You are one of a kind, personally made by God. If you wore a label like the one you have on your shirts, it might say: "Lovingly handmade in Heaven by #1 — God."

How special does it make you feel to know that God himself made you? Share that feeling with your parents.

HOMELESS

Read Matthew 8:19-22.

Jesus said, "I have no place to call home with a bed to sleep in."

Georgia once had a player who was homeless when he was only 9 years old.

Tony Milton was 9 when he left home to live with anybody who would take him in. Still, he starred in football in high school.

When he didn't qualify for a scholarship, he got a job at a hotel. He often had no money and slept in his car. He finally decided to give football another try.

Milton contacted a coach who had recruited him. He was now the first-year head coach at UGA: Mark Richt. He said, "I don't care what I play. I just want a chance to be somebody."

He walked on and made the team. In 2002, he was the number-two tailback behind Musa Smith. In the game against 10th-ranked Tennessee, he ripped off a 25-yard run with 1:43 left that clinched the 18-13 win. The Bulldogs went on to win the SEC championship.

Milton didn't play much his last three years, but he graduated from UGA. His run is now part of Bulldog lore. He is somebody, all right.

You've probably seen them around. The guy with a beard and a backpack at the interstate exit holding a sign. A woman pushing a shopping cart loaded with bags of clothes.

They may be women and children running from violence. They may be army veterans haunted by what they saw in a war. They may be sick or injured workers.

They are the homeless. They have nowhere to live and nowhere to sleep at night.

You are called to feel sorry for them, not to hate them. After all, you serve a Lord — your Jesus — who, like them, had no home.

The homeless, too, are God's children.

Talk to your parents about a way you can help the homeless in your town. Then do it.

A LONG SHOT

Read Matthew 9:9-10.

Jesus said, "Follow me," and Matthew got up and did it.

Talk about a long shot to coach at UGA. She didn't apply for the job and the school was thinking about doing away with her sport altogether. The long shot became one of the greatest coaches in UGA sports history.

She was Suzanne Yoculan. From 1984-2009, she coached the UGA gymnastics team to ten national titles and 16 SEC crowns. She was the National Coach of the Year five times.

Yoculan had no interest in applying for the Georgia job in 1984. For one thing, she wasn't sure there would even be a job there because Georgia was thinking about getting rid of gymnastics. A friend forged her name on an application, so she was surprised when the boss of UGA's women's sports called her up.

Bulldogs

Yoculan didn't even want to visit Athens, but she did. One trip changed her mind. The long shot got the job, and the rest is history.

A long shot is someone or some team that doesn't stand a good chance of doing something. You're a pretty long shot to get married this year or to be named the head gymnastics coach at Georgia.

Matthew was a long shot to be one of Jesus' close friends. He was a tax collector, which meant he was pretty much a crook. He got rich by bullying and stealing from his own people, his own neighbors.

Yet, Jesus said only two words to this lowlife: "Follow me." And Matthew did it.

Like Matthew, we're all long shots to get to Heaven because we can't stand before God with pure, clean hearts. Not unless we do what Matthew did: Get up and follow Jesus. Then we become a sure thing.

Name five things that are long shots in your life. Then name five things that are sure shots.

AS A RULE

Read Matthew 9:10-12.

Some religious leaders complained because Jesus broke the rules and ate with sinners.

Derek Dooley prayed for UGA to slaughter Georgia Tech so his dad would set aside one of his rules.

UGA head football coach Vince Dooley had a rule that none of his kids could go on the sideline during a game until they were 12 years old. When Derek was 7, he asked his dad if he could join him on the field during the Tech game. Coach Dooley said he could if the Dogs were way ahead at the end of the third quarter and Derek didn't bother him.

The night before the game, during the family's prayer time, Derek prayed hard for a Bulldog blowout. His prayers were answered. UGA led 42-7 after three quarters, so his mom took him to the UGA sideline and left him there.

When Tech scored twice, Derek's mom saw father and son talking in violation of the rule the coach had set up for the sideline visit. That night Coach Dooley told her that Derek had said to him, "Dad, don't worry about a thing. Jesus is just having a little fun!"

You live with a whole set of rules, don't you? Go to bed at a certain time. Don't play in the street. Don't be ugly to your brother or sister. Be polite to your teachers.

Rules are hard but they aren't always bad things. Without them, our whole world and our country would be a mess. Nobody would get along, and people couldn't do stuff together.

The rules Jesus didn't like were those that said some people should be treated badly. He broke them, and he expects you to do it, too. You should never mistreat anybody just because somebody says it's the thing to do.

Jesus loves that person. So should you.

Think of a rule that you don't like.
Why do you think you have it?
What would happen if you broke it?

DAY 50

HUMBLE PIE

Read Matthew 23:9-12.

*Those of you who humble
yourselves will be raised up.*

UGA head football coach Vince Dooley once got a double lesson in humility.

Former UGA tennis coach Dan Magill told the story that Coach Dooley once asked him to line him up somebody to play tennis with. Magill came up with a gray-haired senior citizen. "Haven't you got anybody younger?" Dooley asked. Magill just smiled. The senior citizen was the state 70-year-old champion. The UGA head coach didn't win a game off him.

Dooley then insisted he wanted to play somebody younger. This time Magill rounded up a 12-year-old who was small for his age. Again, Dooley didn't like it. "Is this little boy the only player here?" he asked. Perhaps with a smile, Magill said Dooley would get a good workout.

Bulldogs

So the head coach went to the courts and got blitzed by the kid. The boy was the reigning 12-and-under state champion. He would be a two-time All-America at Georgia.

After that, Magill said, Coach Dooley claimed "football knee" in not playing tennis again.

Jesus told us Christians are to be humble. Sometimes it's hard, isn't it, especially since you feel you're pretty good at some things. And Jesus doesn't mind that you pull for the Dawgs and think UGA is Number One.

When Jesus said you are to be humble, he meant you are to be a servant for other people. That means you do nice things for other people. You help someone at school when she needs it. You don't act snooty toward other kids.

But here's something funny. One day, all those who love Jesus will be with him. Then, those who are humble in this life will be the ones whom God will say are the best.

Have you ever thought you were better than someone else? Why? Does God think you're better than someone else?

PROVE IT!

Read Matthew 3:1-6, 13-17.

John told Jesus, "I need to be baptized by you. So why do you come for me to baptize you?"

He was so slow and so small that even Vanderbilt wouldn't let him walk on. So he proved himself at UGA in spectacular fashion.

Nate Taylor wasn't fast and he wasn't big. Everybody said he certainly wasn't good enough to play linebacker at a major college. But Taylor thought he was, and he set out to prove it.

He walked on at Georgia in 1979, a nobody who quickly became somebody. In the game against South Carolina, a bunch of Dawg linebackers got hurt. They had nobody left but Taylor. He "wasn't supposed to be playing, but I ran him in," his coach said. He made 18 tackles. He was so good he received a scholarship the next week. He started every game the rest of his career and led the defense in tackles in both 1979 and 1980. 1980 was the year the Dawgs last won the national title.

Nate Taylor proved that he was good enough.

You know how Nate Taylor felt, don't you? You have to prove yourself over and over again. Every time you take a test, you have to prove you're good enough. Every time you play a sport, you have to prove you're good enough.

But here's something scary: Because you're human and make mistakes, you can never be good enough to measure up to God. Even John the Baptist knew he wasn't good enough, and he was God's chosen prophet and Jesus' cousin.

Here's the way it is. You aren't good enough to get to Heaven without Jesus. You are definitely good enough with him. With Jesus, you have nothing to prove to God.

List some things you have to prove you are good at. Answer this: How can you prove you're good enough to God?

WHAT A SURPRISE!

Read 1 Thessalonians 5:1-6.

The day Jesus comes back should not catch you by surprise.

The Gator head coach's decision surprised his own players, and UGA got a surprise win.

The Dawgs of 1975 were 6-2 but were big underdogs to the Florida Gators. With 3:42 left, Georgia pulled off one the most famous plays in school history. Tight end Richard Appleby threw a bomb to flanker Gene Washington for a touchdown and a 10-7 lead.

The Gators tried to save themselves. They moved to a first down at the Bulldogs 21, but the Dawg defense dug in. Florida wound up with a fourth-and-ten with 50 seconds left. That's when the Gator coach surprised everyone, including his own players.

Everyone expected Florida to go for it since a tie meant they would not win the SEC. At the last minute, the head coach called for a field goal. Caught by surprise, the Gator snapper had not warmed up. The snap was poor, and the kick barely got off the ground.

The Bulldogs had surprised the country.

Is anything much cooler than a surprise birthday party? How much fun would Christmas presents be if they weren't a surprise? Some surprises are about the most fun you can have.

But grown-ups usually spend a lot of time and energy to avoid most surprises. That's because many surprises aren't good things. Avoiding surprises is what adults call planning.

There's one surprise nobody can avoid, how-ever. It's the greatest and most wonderful surprise of all. It's the day Jesus comes back to Earth to take Christians to Heaven.

The Bible tells us you don't know when that will be. It's a surprise. But you can plan for it by loving Jesus and claiming him as your Lord and Savior.

Have you planned for the day Jesus comes back? Tell how you can do that.

DOOR PRIZE

Read Acts 16:6-10.

God kept Paul and his friends
from preaching in Asia Minor.

David Pollack trusted in God, so when a door slammed in his face, he expected another one to open. It did.

Pollack is a Bulldog legend. He was twice the SEC Defensive Player of the Year. He won two awards as the best defensive end in the country.

The Cincinnati Bengals drafted him in the first round of the 2005 NFL draft. He looked forward to a long pro career. Instead, it lasted sixteen games. In the second game of his second pro season, Pollack broke his neck making a tackle. He had surgery and wore a neck brace for months. He never again played the game he loved.

But Pollack wasn't angry, confused, or disappointed by the turn of events in his life. That's because he trusted God to open another door for him.

God did just that. Pollack became an *ESPN* broadcaster with his own TV show. "I feel incredibly blessed to have what I have," he said.

Sometimes you don't get to do the things you want to do the most. It might be a trip to the beach, summer camp, or a special club you wanted to get into.

It's disappointing. You may get confused, too, because you can't see right away what God has in store for you. But you have to be like Paul, who couldn't preach in Asia Minor, and David Pollack, who couldn't play pro football anymore.

What you need to do is to always trust in God. You know he has something for you. Most of the time, it's something greater than you could have imagined.

When God closes a window, he opens a door.

Draw an open door. On it, list some things that you wanted and you got. Then thank God for those blessings.

POP THE QUESTION

Read Matthew 16:13-17.

Jesus asked his disciples, "Who do you think I am?"

Joe Burson had a question at halftime for a Bulldog coach. The answer was a good one.

1962 was not a good year for UGA football, and Auburn was a heavy favorite to beat the Dawgs. Sure enough, the Tigers led 14-7 at halftime.

In the locker room, Burson, a defensive back, had a question for his position coach. He asked if he could gamble and go for an interception on a certain play. The coach said he could but that he couldn't try it unless he were sure he could get the ball.

Georgia rallied to tie the game. A field goal in the fourth quarter gave UGA a 17-14 lead. All the while, Burson thought about the answer to his question and waited.

With 8:21 to play, he pulled off one of the most memorable plays in Bulldog history. He gambled on the interception, got it, and sped 87 yards for a touchdown.

Georgia pulled off the upset 30-21.

In school, others have questions for you. Outside school, you have questions for others. Hey, what's for supper? Can I go outside and play? When are we going on vacation? What kind of team will Georgia have this year?

Some questions aren't really a big deal. One question, though, is the most important one you will ever ask and answer. It's the one that Jesus asked Peter: "Who do you say I am?" Peter gave the one and only correct answer: "Jesus, you are the Son of God."

Why is that question so important that it is the only one that matters? The answer decides how you spend your life — walking with Jesus — and how you spend all of eternity — living with Jesus.

Tell your parents in your words the answer to this question: Who is Jesus?

BLESS YOU

Read Ephesians 1:3-8.

*In Jesus, God has blessed us
with every spiritual blessing.*

Who ever knew that stopping to fill up with gas could turn into a great blessing for Georgia's football program?

In the summer of 1939, Bill Hartman, UGA's backfield coach, took a recruiting trip to Ohio. It wasn't a good trip. He arrived at his destination to find out the player he wanted had decided to go to Ohio State.

On his way out of town, Hartman stopped to fill up his car for the drive home. He talked to a guy at the station who told him the best back in the state lived right down the street.

Hartman turned around and drove until he found the player's house. His father was sitting on the front porch. Before Hartman left, the player agreed to take a trip to Athens.

Bulldogs

The player was Frank Sinkwich, one of the greatest players in college football history. A running back, he was the first player from the South to win the Heisman Trophy (1942). He was a two-time All-America and was inducted into the college hall of fame in 1954.

Like Coach Bill Hartman, you never know where you will find blessings in life. At home, on the playground, in the classroom, at the swimming pool. Who knows?

What you can know is that God is always at work preparing blessings just for you. If you will trust in him and obey him, he will pour out those blessings on you.

While God wants only what is good for you, he doesn't manage a candy store. That means he won't bail you out when you make a bad decision or do something wrong. Instead, he will let you learn a lesson from your mistake.

But even that is a blessing. If you do learn, you'll never do it again. You'll be smarter. Even when you're crying, God blesses you.

Make a list of ten blessings in your life.

LAUGH IT UP

Read Genesis 21:3-7.

Sarah said, "God has given me laughter, and others will laugh with me."

Head coach Vince Dooley's talks to his team the day before a game were always real serious. Until the time one player turned it into a comedy routine.

Cornerback Greg Bell could do a dead-on impression of the head Dawg. He knew, as all the players did, that Dooley always used a big board to write his key points on. And he always gave the same speech.

Before the 1978 game with Georgia Tech, Dooley was held up doing TV interviews. So Bell did a Dooley routine. He wrote words like "No Mistakes" on the board and imitated Dooley perfectly. The players fell out laughing.

The coach didn't stand a chance. When he

showed up, right on cue, right where Bell had written it, he wrote "No Mistakes." Then he said exactly what Bell had said. The players went berserk with laughter.

When the coach wrote "Point No. 2" right where Bell had written it, the room fell apart with laughter. Dooley had no choice but to give up. He yelled, "Y'all know what to do, and you better do it tomorrow." End of meeting.

What makes you laugh? Is it someone at school who tells funny stories or makes funny faces? Or someone who can imitate a teacher?

Adults don't laugh as much as kids do, but even kids don't laugh enough. It seems the world is just too serious.

We all need to remember as Sarah did that one of God's best gifts to us is laughter. The greatest gift of all is Jesus, and that's reason enough to laugh. Because of Jesus, you can laugh at the world's pain.

The tears you cry will pass. But your laughter, which comes from God, will remain forever.

***Try to make somebody laugh by telling
a funny story or doing a funny dance.***

FUSSBUDGETS

Read Philippians 2:14-16.

*Do everything without complaining
or arguing.*

Lamar "Racehorse" Davis started to complain when he got the wrong shoes, but he didn't. He got a scholarship because of it.

A high school senior in 1939, Davis was invited to play in an all-star basketball game in Atlanta. When his turn came for equipment, the game sponsors had run out of basketball shoes. They simply handed him a pair of football shoes.

Davis thought of complaining to his coach, but decided not to. An all-star football game was to be played also, so he figured he'd just play in that. In the game, he returned a punt for a touchdown. A UGA coach in the stands saw it and offered him a football scholarship.

Davis scored what some writers have called

Bulldogs

the most dramatic touchdown in UGA history. In 1941 against Auburn, Georgia got the ball with three seconds left in a scoreless game. Davis caught a pass and went 65 yards for a touchdown and a 7-0 Bulldog win.

He wound up in the College Football Hall of Fame. All of it may never have happened had Davis complained about his shoes.

When somebody does us wrong, our first response is to fuss and complain. Paul tells us not to. What's up with that?

Paul says that when you fuss, you're not acting the way Jesus would. Especially when you are real nasty to someone else. But if you don't complain, you're shining Jesus to that other person. God himself can brag about you to the angels in Heaven.

What should you do? Say a little prayer for patience and forget about it. You then walk away blameless before God. Now it's the other person who has something to complain about.

Before a mirror, pretend someone has done you wrong. Say a prayer for patience and watch yourself walk away.

DAY 58

WISE GUYS

Read James 3:13-17.

You show your wisdom by living a good life and doing good deeds.

In their wisdom, Chick-fil-A bigwigs thought they had come up with a great promotion for their bowl game. Uh — no.

Georgia met Virginia in the 1998 Chick-fil-A Peach Bowl. To highlight the occasion, the company decided to give every spectator a toy cow. A plush little black-and-white cow was placed in the cup holder of every seat.

All that sounded like genius. And then UVa scored a touchdown. About 1,000 very unhappy Dawg fans threw their cows onto the field. When a message on the video board asked fans not to toss their cows, the response was more airborne toys.

The cows kept flying as Virginia jumped out to a 21-0 lead. But Georgia rallied to lead

35-27 with 7:01 left. Now Virginia fans were tossing their cows. With 19 seconds left, UVa missed a field goal and UGA won 35-33.

Anyone who still had his cow sailed it into the air, Virginia fans because they were unhappy, UGA fans in celebration.

As it was with the fiasco of the flying cows, what appears to be smart sometimes isn't.

The world finds its wisdom in places such as the classrooms of your school, the offices of business leaders, or the movies Hollywood puts out. Wisdom for the world often means loading up on a whole bunch of stuff. True wisdom, though, is found in the Bible.

Jesus said the way the world sees wisdom is nothing but foolishness. Instead, Jesus said, the wise person lives a life filled with good deeds and mercy toward others.

In other words, you're really wise only when you love Jesus and live how he wants you to.

List five ways the world says you show wisdom. Then list five ways Jesus says you show wisdom.

IT'S THE TRUTH

Read Matthew 5:33-37.

Jesus said, "If you mean 'yes,' say 'yes.' If you mean 'no,' say 'no.'"

A lot of far-fetched stories have been told about the great UGA running back Herschel Walker. At least one of them is true: He never worked out with weights.

When he was 12, Herschel started doing push-ups and sit-ups and running sprints every day. Within a year, he had done more than 100,000 push-ups and sit-ups and run more than a million yards. He never stopped doing this, even when he was on the high school football team.

By the time he was 17, he had a body that most body builders would die for. One reason he never lifted weights was that his little high school didn't have any. When they did get a few weights, Walker grabbed a 250-lb. barbell and pumped it a few times. "Coach, 250 ain't heavy," he said. He never lifted another weight.

But all the Bulldogs lift weights. When he came to Athens, Herschel was tested for his strength as all the players are. One coach said he was as strong as a thousand-dollar mule already. The coaches decided Herschel didn't need to lift weights. So he didn't — and never did. It's the truth.

The truth is that you probably don't tell the truth all the time. Sometimes you may lie to avoid hurting someone else's feelings. Or to make yourself look better to someone you want to impress. Or to get out of trouble.

But Jesus says you are always to tell the truth. As far as Jesus is concerned, telling the truth is right; lying is wrong.

Lying is what the devil ("the evil one") does. God cannot lie; the devil lies as a way of life. Whose side are you on when you tell a lie?

Recall a lie you told to get out of trouble. Did it make you feel good? Do you think God was proud of you for lying?

GEORGIA
DAY 60

BLOOD TYPE

Read Hebrews 9:19-22.

Without the shedding of blood, no one can be forgiven.

The Dawgs used to have a coach who really did shed his blood for the Red and Black.

He was defensive coordinator Erk Russell, who went on to become the first head football coach at Georgia Southern.

Russell was a master motivator. He called his defense the "Junkyard Dawgs" and got the Redcoat Band to play "Bad, Bad Leroy Brown" when the defense made a big play.

His masterpiece, the one that made him a Bulldog legend, was an accident. In the late 1970s before a game, he would butt his players' shoulder pads with his bald head. A player new to the defense didn't know the drill, so he crashed into Erk's head with his helmet. Blood streamed all down the coach's face.

The sight of that blood drove the players into a total frenzy. They went nuts. Both a tradition and a legend were born that day. After that, Russell always butted a player's helmet before a game to make his head bleed.

God is not at all like you. The Bible tells us that God's ways are not your ways. One way that's true is that God requires the spilling of blood before he will forgive you for your sins.

Before Jesus, that meant killing animals such as goats and pigeons and sprinkling the blood around. How weird is that?

Jesus' death on the cross began the New Covenant, but it wasn't the end of God's demand for blood to be shed. So why don't you have to kill a bird and then spread the blood all around your church? How do you get forgiveness by praying for it in Jesus' name?

It's because Jesus shed his blood for you on the cross. You have Jesus, not pigeons.

Draw a picture of Jesus on the cross to help you remember the blood he shed for you so you can be forgiven.

DAY 61

DRY RUN

Read 1 Kings 16:29-30; 17:1; 18:1.

*Elijah told Ahab, "There won't be
any rain for the next few years."*

The Bulldog drought was longer than the one God and Elijah laid on Israel. It lasted eight years.

From 1949 through 1956, Georgia Tech beat Georgia eight straight times in football. The drought was broken in 1957 by a team led by fullback Theron Sapp.

In 1954, Sapp injured his neck in a diving accident before he ever played a down for the Dawgs. Doctors told him he would never play football again.

He refused to believe it. He wore a cast his freshman year, played on the B-team as a sophomore, and then had another injury his junior year.

But in 1957, he was healthy. The game was

scoreless in the third quarter when Sapp carried the ball six straight times from the 26-yard-line. On fourth down from the 1, he scored. Georgia won 7-0, and Sapp became known as "The Man Who Broke the Drought."

If you live in the South, you know a little something about drought, don't you? It gets really hot down here, and sometimes in the summer you probably don't get a whole lot of rain in your hometown.

The sun bakes everything, including the concrete that gets so hot it burns your feet. Ever seen a truck with "Wash Me" written on the back windshield?

God put in you a physical thirst for water to keep you alive. But he also put a spiritual thirst in you. Without God, we are like a dried-up pond. There's no life, only death.

There's only one fountain to go to and drink all you want of the true water of life: Jesus.

Fill an empty water bottle with sand to remind you how a soul looks without God: all dried up and dead.

THE BAD GUYS

Read Ephesians 6:10-13.

*For Christians, the bad guys are
not humans but spiritual forces of
evil and the powers of darkness.*

Some Georgia fans were on their way home from a football game when somebody tried to kill them.

In 1900, Georgia played Sewanee in Atlanta. A bunch of Bulldog fans took the train to the game. As they headed home, they didn't know four men had decided to wreck the train. The crooks planned to derail it and then rob the passengers and the baggage and mail cars.

One of the bad guys — probably the dumbest one — had boasted about their plans. Thus, police officers caught them in the act. They warned the train with a lantern, and it stopped short of the bridge where the tracks had been torn up by two of the criminals.

Bulldogs

The handcuffed men were brought onto the train to take to jail. When the Bulldog fans heard about what they had tried to do, they wanted to beat them up. But the tracks were soon repaired and the train went on its way.

The bad guys wound up in jail, and all those Bulldog fans had a great story to tell.

Evil is all around us. It's the really, really bad stuff that goes on in the world.

But evil isn't something God created. When he finished making the world, God pronounced it good. Evil comes from the spirit world, from Satan and his flunkies.

You are part of a struggle that stretches all across the universe, a battle between good and evil. The fight is for your soul. Giving your life to Jesus puts you on the side of good.

One day, Jesus will come back and defeat evil for all times. Only goodness will survive. Thus, one thing is sure: Evil is for losers.

With an adult's help, pick three examples from today's news of evil and three of good. Talk about why they're different.

THE NEW YOU

Read 2 Corinthians 5:15-18.

The moment you believe in Christ,
you are a new person.

Georgia's first basketball All-America was on loan from the football team.

Joe "Zippy" Morocco's first love was basketball, but in 1948 UGA didn't hand out basketball scholarships. So he played football and then made himself over into a basketball player once the season ended.

It wasn't easy. He said it was tough physically changing sports. He said the two sports actually used different muscles. But he was very good at both. He averaged nearly ten yards every time he touched the football.

The NFL's Philadelphia Eagles drafted him after the 1952 season, but he decided to stay at UGA and play basketball for one more year.

With no football to play, he was great. He

scored more points than any player in SEC history. He was named the SEC's most valuable player, the first Bulldog ever to earn that honor. He was also named All-America.

UGA has had many athletes who made themselves over by playing two sports, but Zippy Morocco remains among the best.

Have you ever seen one of those TV shows where they take someone, buy them some clothes, and redo their hair and makeup? It's called a makeover. It makes them look like a new person. But they're not a new person.

Those changes are on the outside. When you get a haircut or get a new pair of jeans, you're still the same person, aren't you?

If you really want to be a new person, you have to change in the inside, in your heart. The only way that can be done is with Jesus. You become a new person when you do things to please Jesus and not other people.

List some ways you can change the way you look. Then list some ways you can change how you act with Jesus' help.

COMEBACK KID

Read Acts 9:18-22.

Those who heard Paul asked, "Isn't he the one who persecuted and killed Christians in Jerusalem?"

He lost his scholarship. Then he was in a car wreck and was told he wouldn't play football again. Only a few months later, he made the biggest play in the history of Georgia football.

Receiver Lindsay Scott had his scholarship taken away after he got into an argument with a coach and shoved him. "I hated myself for what I had done," Scott later said.

Then that summer he was driving home when he wrecked his car. He had a concussion and three broken bones in his foot. A doctor told his mom his football career was over.

But Lindsay Scott was determined to make a comeback. So on Nov. 8, 1980, he started when Georgia played Florida. Florida led 21-20 with less than two minutes to play. Quarterback Buck Belue threw a short pass to Scott, and he outran the Florida defense for a 93-yard touchdown. The miraculous comeback sent the Bulldogs on their way to the national title.

A comeback means you come from behind. You know by now that you don't always win. You make an A on a test one day and sprain your ankle the next. You do all your chores at home but get in trouble for talking in class.

In life, even for a kid, winning isn't about never losing. Things will go wrong for you sometimes. Winning means you pick yourself up from your defeat and keep going. You make a comeback of your own, just the way Paul and Lindsay Scott did.

Besides, God's grace is always there for you, so your comeback can always be bigger than your setback. With Jesus in your life, it's not how you start that counts; it's how you finish.

Remember a time a team you like made a comeback. Compare that to a time you came back when something went wrong.

FAMILY MEN

Read Mark 3:31-35.

Jesus said, "Whoever does God's will is my family."

Twins Jonas and Jarvis Hayes are so close that once when Jonas got hurt in a game, it was Jarvis who vomited.

"He's my brother, man," Jarvis explained. This was after he had visited a trash can at half-time of a Georgia basketball game in 2001. He had been sickened by seeing Jonas' dislocated finger.

It was always about family for the Hayes twins. Out of high school, they insisted they would play college basketball together. They went to Western Carolina, which is in North Carolina, but then the coach was fired. Their dad picked up the phone and called UGA. "I've got these two sons from Atlanta who want to come home," he said. But only if Georgia had

Bulldogs

scholarships for both of them.

The Dawgs did, and so two of the most popular players in UGA basketball history came to Athens. They were both really good basketball players, but they were family men first.

Somebody once said that families are like fudge, mostly sweet with a few nuts. You can probably name your sweet kinfolks — and the nutty ones, too.

You may not like it all the time, but you have a family. You can blame God for that. God loves the idea of family so much that he chose to live in one as a son, a brother, and a cousin. Jesus had a family.

But Jesus also had a new definition for what makes up a family. It's not just blood. It's a choice. Everybody who does God's will is a member of Jesus' family.

That includes you. You have family members all over the place who stand ready to love you because you're all part of God's big family.

With help from a parent or grandparent, draw your family tree.

SLUGGING IT OUT

Read Hebrews 12:14-15.

Do all you can to live in peace with everyone.

A Georgia football player once slugged it out with a coach from the other team.

Harold Ketron was a Bulldog lineman who lettered in 1901-03 and 1906. He was so good an Atlanta sportswriter once said, "Ketron is a whole team in himself."

For "War Eagle" Ketron, no football game was complete without a good fist-fight. One of his favorite techniques was to grab his man by the hair and spit tobacco into his eyes. The angry opponent would often swing at Ketron. Since the refs couldn't see the spit that started the fray, Ketron's victim would get the penalty.

In the 1903 Vanderbilt game, a Commodore coach kept running onto the field to tell the referees to watch the UGA star closely. Finally,

Ketron had all he could take so he took a swing at the coach. A fight broke out with Ketron and the coach slugging away at each other.

Since the game was played in Atlanta, "War Eagle" stayed in the game. The Vandy coach was arrested and hauled off to jail.

It's a good thing that football players today don't fight the way they did in Harold Ketron's day. That doesn't mean players don't get mad.

Have you ever played in a game of some kind where someone from the other team hurt you? You probably got mad, didn't you?

Anger is all right; it's a healthy response as long as you keep it under control. But fighting is never the right answer. It's not just because you make an enemy but also because Jesus said you should make peace instead of fighting.

Making peace often isn't as easy as taking a swing, but it requires more courage. It's also exactly what Jesus would do.

Is there someone at school you don't get along with? Try talking to that person and making him or her your friend.

DAY 67

PAIN RELIEF

Read 2 Corinthians 1:3-7.

*God is the father of all comfort in
our pain and our suffering.*

There's just no way you can pull off a gymnastics routine with a broken toe. Too much pain. Unless you're a Georgia Bulldog and your team needs you to win the SEC championship.

In 1991, Alabama and Georgia were neck-in-neck for the title. The GymDogs had the floor exercise still to do. They had only five gymnasts since Lisa Alicea had a broken toe. She didn't even warm up.

When a Georgia gymnast fell, the Alabama team started celebrating. A gymnast short because of the injury, Georgia had to count the low score that came with the fall.

Hold on. Coach Suzanne Yoculan said she was never sure why, but she had listed the injured Alicea in the lineup. She could compete,

Bulldogs

even with her broken toe.

Still, it was a long shot. Alicea hadn't competed in weeks, and the pain would be awful. Alicea performed with gritted teeth it hurt so bad. But she nailed her routine.

Her score meant the GymDogs had won the SEC championship. That didn't hurt at all.

Does a day go by when you don't feel pain? A scrape from a fall on the playground. A blister from your shoes. A bump on the head.

Some pain isn't just physical. Bruises and bumps don't hurt nearly as bad as it does when your dog dies or someone is mean to you.

Jesus knows all about pain. After all, they drove nails into his hands and feet, hung him on two pieces of wood, and stuck a spear in his side. It was an awful, painful way to die.

So when you hurt, you can find comfort in Jesus. He's been there before. He knows all about tears and pain.

Look over your body for bumps, bruises, scratches, and scrapes. Tell how you got each one and how bad it hurt.

MIDDLE OF NOWHERE

Read Genesis 28:10-16.

Jacob woke up and said to himself, "The Lord is in this place, and I didn't even know it."

Right smack dab in the middle of nowhere, a traveling salesman found one of UGA's greatest athletes ever.

In 1928, an ice-cream salesman couldn't find Carnesville, Ga. He sat in his car at an intersection, trying to figure out where to go. A boy was plowing a cotton field beside the road, so he asked the youngster for directions.

To the salesman's surprise, the boy picked up the plow with one arm and pointed toward Carnesville. Impressed, the salesman, a Bulldog fan, talked to the boy. He learned the plowboy had been a star in football, baseball, and track in high school. Clemson had offered him a football scholarship.

Bulldogs

The salesman reported his find to Georgia's head football coach, who contacted the boy. He turned Clemson down and came to Athens. His name was Spurgeon Chander.

Chandler starred as the left halfback for the Dawgs for three seasons and was the team's punter and played defense. He also was the ace pitcher for the UGA baseball team.

Did you know there's a town in Georgia named Shoulderbone? And one called Talking Rock? There's even one named Between. And another called Barney.

They're little places, not on an interstate highway. They're in the middle of nowhere.

But don't get those towns wrong. They are special and wonderful. That's because God is in Welcome, Ga., and in Youth, Ga., just like he is in Athens and Atlanta.

As Jacob found out one morning, the middle of nowhere is holy ground — because God is there.

Find some funny names of towns on a Georgia map. Remind yourself God is in each one of them.

PEACE TREATY

Read Matthew 5:23-24.

Go and make peace with anyone you're angry with.

Georgia and Georgia Tech students once signed a peace treaty, promising no guns and no laxatives during a game.

Back in 1919, baseball was the big sport between the two schools. In a game, Tech's pep band left the stands and cranked up full blast to try to shake up the Bulldog pitcher. It didn't work; Georgia won 2-1. The students did a lot of pushing, shoving, and name-calling.

The next day, the Dawg pitcher embarrassed Tech with an 8-0 no-hitter. Behavior and anger got worse. Fights and brawls broke out everywhere in the stands and then in Atlanta that night. Something had to be done before somebody got hurt really bad.

So leaders from the two schools met and

Bulldogs

drew up a peace treaty. They promised not to shoot the players from the other school during a game. They also promised they wouldn't poison the other team's players by dropping laxatives into their water buckets.

Part of the fun of college sports and being a Bulldog fan is making fun of and insulting fans from Auburn or Florida or Tech or Tennessee. It's fun because it's not really serious. As long as the teams play each other, you'll keep digging at folks who are fans of one of the Dawgs' rivals. You don't ever make peace.

It's different with your friends and family members. When you have a spat with them, you need to make up. You make your own personal peace treaty by saying you're sorry.

Jesus tells us that you are to offer a hand and a hug to a person you've said ugly things to or had a fight with. Saying "I'm sorry" gets you right with that person and right with God.

Think up a time recently when you were ugly to a family member. Tell them you're sorry and offer them a hug.

WHO, ME?

Read Judges 6:12-16.

*"Lord," Gideon asked, "how can I
save Israel? I'm a nobody even in
my own family."*

A defensive tackle once played some at quarterback for Georgia in a bowl game.

George Patton was an All-American defensive tackle in 1965 and '66 and was All-SEC three times. In high school, he was "a slow quarterback with a strong arm." Patton said he knew a whole lot of schools weren't looking for "a quarterback with no foot speed."

When UGA head coach Vince Dooley asked Patton if he wanted to move from quarterback to defense, he didn't hesitate.

In 1966, Patton's senior season, the Dawgs won the SEC and whipped up on SMU 24-9 in the Cotton Bowl. Late in the game, Patton thought Dooley was kidding when the coach

Bulldogs

ordered him to go into the game and play a series at quarterback. He wasn't joking.

Patton told his receivers "to run as far and as fast as they could" and he was going to chunk it as far and as hard as he could. He did just that, sailing three long incomplete passes.

You ever said, "Who, me?" as George Patton did when the coach told him to go play quarterback? Maybe when the teacher called on you in class? Or when somebody asked you to sing a solo? Your stomach kind of knots up, doesn't it? You get real nervous, too.

That's the way Gideon felt when God called on him to lead his people in battle. And you might feel exactly the same way when somebody calls on you to say a prayer. Or to read a part in Sunday school.

Hey, I can't do that, you might say. But you can. God wants you to do stuff for him. Like Gideon, God thinks you can do it just fine. And with God's help, you will. Just like Gideon.

Think of some ways you can help at Sunday school and then volunteer.

NOTES

(by devotion number)

1   All the school had was . . . the rules of football.: John F. Stegeman, *The Ghosts of Herty Field* (Athens: The University of Georgia Press, 1997), pp. 2-3.

2   "It's the best feeling I've ever had," Chip Towers, "Redemption," *Online Athens.com*. Nov. 17, 1996, http://www.onlineathens.com/1996/111796/1117.dogs.html.

3   The surprised South Carolina . . . couldn't believe it either.: Rob Suggs, *Top Dawg* (Nashville: Thomas Nelson, 2008), p. 118.

4   "I freaked out,": Roger Clarkson, "UGA's Earls on Road to Recovery," *OnlineAthens.com*, July 4, 2011, http://www.onlineathens.com/stories/070411/gym_85236044.shtml.

5   Late in the game . . . for a touchdown.: Loran Smith with Lewis Grizzard, *Glory! Glory!* (Atlanta: Peachtree Publishers Limited, 1981), p. 6.

6   The band started in . . . up with more money: "The History of the University of Georgia Redcoat Band 1905-2005," http://www.bands.music.uga.edu/redcoat/history.php.

7   In the middle of the . . . stadium on this site.": Tim Hix, *Stadium Stories: Georgia Bulldogs* (Guilford, CN: The Globe Pequot Press, 2006), pp. 107-08.

8   Back in the 1930s . . .snakes never did fight: Dan Magill, *Dan Magill's Bull-Doggerel* (Atlanta: Longstreet Press, Inc., 1993), pp. 157-60.

9   Lineman Tim Morrison was . . . game for the kick.: Tony Barnhart, *What It Means to Be a Bulldog* (Chicago: Triumph Books, 2004), p. 271.

10 "We were just getting it handed to us,": Barnhart, *What It Means to Be a Bulldog*, p. 334.

11 When the season ended, . . . saved his daughter's life.: Suzanne Yoculan and Bill Donaldson, *Perfect 10* (Athens: Hill Street Press, 2006), pp. 76-82.

12 Quarterback Kirby Moore didn't . . . run it. Flea Flicker!": Barnhart, *What It Means to Be a Bulldog*, p. 124.

13 Five senior football players . . . together on the field: *Echoes of Georgia Football*, ed. Ken Samelson (Chicago: Triumph books, 2006), pp. 162-68.

14 In 1995, Glamour magazine . . . College Women of America.: Dave Kindred, "Germ Study a Model Role for Volleyball 'Gym Rat,'" *The Atlanta Journal/The Atlanta Constitution*, Jan. 21, 1996, p. E3.

14 "I love pathogens," . . . I'll do it,": Kindred, "Germ Study."

15 "You're going to have to win this ballgame.": Jonathan Branch, "Football Notebook: QB Murray Gets First Win," *DOGbytesonline.com*, Oct. 27, 2012, http://www.dogbytesonline.com/football-notebook-qb-murray-gets-first-win.

16 The ball was shaped like . . . couldn't throw it.: Clyde Bolton, *The Crimson Tide* (Huntsville, AL: The Strode Publishers, 1972), p. 46.

16 Fans ran onto the . . . way of the players.: Clyde Bolton, *War Eagle* (Huntsville, AL: The Strode Publishers, 1973), p. 49.

16 Players had long hair . . . didn't have helmets.: Bolton, *War Eagle*, p. 45.

16 There were no scoreboards.: Bolton, *War Eagle*, p. 69.

16   The fields didn't have . . . play after dark.: Bolton, *War Eagle*, p. 48.

16   The halves were as long . . . wanted them to be.: Bolton, *War Eagle*, p. 80.

16   Teammates dragged the . . . down the field.: Bolton, *War Eagle*, p. 81.

16   One time a Georgia . . . caught a pass.: Bolton, *The Crimson Tide*, p. 37.

17   Kim Thompson was so . . . because of her uniform.: Lya Wodraska, "No Skirting the Issue at UGA," *The Atlanta Journal/The Atlanta Constitution*, Jan. 20, 1993, p. F7.

17   Kim Thompson played . . .the Lord to keep,": Wodraska, "No Skirting."

18   the players ate anywhere . . . they couldn't go anymore.: Stegeman, p. 53.

18   The football players even . . . was in a basement.: Stegeman, p. 54

18   the site where they . . . an old red dirt field.: Stegeman, p. 38.

22   In the 1920s, a . . . "Put him to work.": Magill, p. 176.

23   Some fans had brought . . . band threw him off,: Vince Dooley with Loran Smith, *Dooley's Dawgs* (Atlanta, Longstreet Press, 2003), p. 69

23   Next week, the awful . . . the Chattahoochee River.: Vince Dooley with Loran Smith, p. 70.

24   he could kick out light bulbs in the ceiling.: Magill, p. 55.

24   On one trip, he . . . for a little while.: Magill, p. 59.

25   Two weeks before the . . . 5:45 in the morning!: Josh Kendall, "Moreno, Teammates Mount Day-Long Georgia Celebration," *The Telegraph*, Oct. 28, 2007, p. 1C.

26   After the tough loss, . . . paid $1 a bushel for.: Bill Cromartie, *Clean Old-Fashioned Hate* (Huntsville, AL: The Strode Publishers, 1977), p. 34.

26   Late in the 1942 Orange . . . running all down his face!: Jesse Outlar, *Between the Hedges* (Huntsville, AL: The Strode Publishers, 1974), p. 67.

27   his family came to . . . new school was lunch.: Smith with Grizzard, p. 83.

28   It looked as though . . . short of the goal line.: Smith with Grizzard, p. 7.

29   The Georgia mascot for . . . field before the game.: Stegeman, p. 5.

29   After Georgia won the . . . even rode the goat.: Stegeman, p. 7.

29   He wore a black . . . on each side.: Magill, p. 175.

29   He also had on a . . . from the Georgia crowd.: Stegeman, p. 11.

30   A Missouri player had . . . the player said that.: Marc Weizner, "Missouri DT Gets in First Verbal Jabs," *DOGbytesonline.com*, Sept. 3, 2012, http://www.dogbytesonline.com/mizzou-dt-gets-in-first-verbal-jabs.

30   Even head coach's mother didn't like it.: Marc Weizner, "Quick Hits: Dawson Yet to Meet with NCAA," *DOGbytesonline.com*, Sept. 5, 2012, http://www.dogbytesonline.com/quick-hits-dawson-yet-to-meet.

30   Quarterback Aaron Murray said the insult helped fire the team up.: Marc Weizner, "Welcome to the SEC," *DOGbytesonline.com*, Sept. 9, 2012, http://www.dogbytesonline.com/welcome-to-the-sec.

30   In the excited Georgia . . . "Grown Man Football.": Marc Weizner, "Dogs Showed 'Mental, Physical Toughness in Win," *DOGbytesonline.com*, Sept. 9, 2012. htttp://www.dogbytesonline.com/dogs-showed-mental-physical-toughness-in-win.

31   Georgia punted one time . . . signaled touchdown!: Stegeman, pp. 71-73.

32   One of Georgia's greatest . . . in the Ocmulgee River.: Magill, p. 21.

32   He then stole the . . .shoot the free throws: Magill, p. 21.

33   *Sports Illustrated* pretty much . . . to play the game.: Franz Lidz, "Mirror, Mirror," *Sports Illustrated*, Nov. 15, 1999, htttp://www.sportsillustrated.

cnn.com/vault/article/magazine/MAG1017687/index.htm.

33   They used their own . . . How'd they do that?": Lidz, "Mirror, Mirror."

34   he didn't really know . . . made up his mind.: Barnhart, *What It Means to Be a Bulldog*, pp. 188-89.

35   something was wrong . . . his life to Jesus.: Chris Arnzen, "Alec Millen," *Iron Sharpens Iron*, Nov. 19, 2008, sharpens.blogsports.com/2008/11/mp3-available-here_19.html.

36   happy Bulldog fans by . . . Between the Hoses.": Patrick Garbin, *"Then Vince Said to Herschel . . ."* (Chicago: Triumph Books, 2007), p. 198.

37   He was given a . . . He was a Bulldog!: Chris Starrs, "UGA Snapper Frix Has a Story to Tell," *DOGbytesonline.com*, Dec. 29, 2012, http://www.dogbytesonline.com/uga-snapper-frix-has-a-story-to-tell.

38   330-lb. lineman Chester . . . bottom of that dogpile.: Vince Dooley, *Dooley's Play Book* (Athens: Hill Street Press, 2008), p. 137.

39   he said the most . . . in five seasons.: Vince Dooley with Blake Giles, *Tales from the 1980 Georgia Bulldogs* (Champaign, IL: Sports Publishing L.L.C., 2005), p. 103.

39   He once rappelled off . . . by campus police.: Dooley with Giles, p. 104.

39   Steele was a leader . . . "He is my hero.": Dooley with Giles, p. 105.

40   One evening, after he . . . wanted him to.: Suggs, pp. 150-51.

41   when the UGA president . . . he forgot his name!: Dooley with Smith, p. 2

41   The next week some . . . "What did you expect?": Dooley with Smith, p. 8.

42   His mother had to . . . at football and basketball.: Roger Clarkson, "Big Man, Big Plans," *DOGBytesonline.com*, Oct. 19, 2012, http://www.dogbytesonline.com/big-man-big-plans.

43   She showed up for . . . she wore red.: Scott Bernarde, "UGA Equestrian Team Set to Defend National Title," *Atlanta Journal-Constitution*, March 25, 2010, http://www.ajc.com/sports/uga/uga-equestrian-team.

44   UGA called time out . . . sent him into the game.: Barnhart, *What It Means to Be a Bulldog*, pp. 234-35.

45   Center Ben Jones said . . . smile all the time,": Roger Clarkson, "Dogs' Gentle Giant," *DOGBytesonline.com*, Aug 9, 2011, http://www.dogbytesonline.com/dogs-gentle-giant-47490.

46   little UGA III stood right . . . "We got 'em tonight,": Ron Higgins, "SEC Traditions: Uga VIII," *SEC Digital Network*, Oct. 22, 2010, http://www.secdigitalnetowkr.com/SECNation/SECTraditions/tabid/1073/Article/21644.

47   Tony Milton was 9 . . . to be somebody.": Garbin, p. 233.

48   Yoculan had no interest . . . trip changed her mind.: Yoculan and Donaldson, pp. 40-42.

49   UGA head football coach . . . having a little fun!": Ron Higgins, "SEC Traditions: The Dooley Family Tree," *SEC Digital Network*, Sept. 2, 2010, http://www.secdigitalnetwork.com/SECNation/SECTraditions/tabid/1073/Article/134279.

50   Former UGA tennis coach . . . not playing tennis again.: Magill, pp. 137-38.

51   In the game against . . . I ran him in.": Dooley with Giles, p. 76.

52   Caught by surprise, . . . not warmed up.: Garbin, p. 151.

53   Pollack wasn't angry, . . . have what I have,": Ron Higgins, "SEC Traditions: Pollack is Still a Showstopper," *SEC Digital Network*, Dec. 9, 2011, http://www.secdigitalnetwork.com/SECNation/SECTraditions/tabid/1073/Article/229991.

54 In the locker room, . . . could get the ball.: Garbin, p. 110.
55 In the summer of 1939, . . . a trip to Athens.: *Echoes of Georgia Football*, pp. 47-48.
56 Cornerback Greg Bell could . . . better do it tomorrow.: Dooley with Giles, pp. 156-57.
57 When his turn came . . . he'd just play in that.: Loran Smith, *Wally's Boys* (Athens, Longstreet Press, 2005), p. 48.
58 the company decided to . . . more airborne toys.: Garbin, p. 224.
58 Anyone who still had his cow sailed it into the air,: Garbin, p. 225.
59 When he was 12, . . . need to lift weights.: Terry Todd, "My Body's Like an Army," *Sports Illustrated*, Oct. 4, 1982, http://sportsillustrated.cnn.com/vault/article/magazine/MAG1125982/index.htm.
60 In the late 1970s . . .They went nuts.: Hix, p. 5.
62 In 1900, Georgia played . . . went on its way.: Stegeman, pp. 55-57.
63 He said it was . . . used different muscles.: Tim Hix, *Hoop Tales: Georgia Bulldogs Men's Basketball* (Guilford, CN: The Globe Pequot Press, 2006).
64 "I hated myself for what I had done,": Smith with Grizzard, p. 116.
65 "He's my brother" . . . Jonas' dislocated finger.: Hix, *Hoop Tales*, p. 95.
65 Out of high school, . . . basketball together.: Hix, *Hoop Tales*, p. 99.
65 Their dad picked up . . . for both of them.: Hix, *Hoop Tales*, p. 94.
66 "Ketron is a whole team in himself.": Stegeman, p. 63.
66 For "War Eagle" Ketron . . . a good fist-fight.: Stegeman, p. 61.
66 One of his favorite . . . hauled off to jail.: Stegeman, p. 63.
67 In 1991, Alabama and . . . hurt so bad.: Yoculan and Donaldson, pp. 29-30.
68 In 1928, an ice-cream . . . was Spurgeon Chandler.: Magill, p. 18.
69 Tech's pep band left . . . into their water buckets.: Cromartie, pp. 86-87.
70 "a slow quarterback with . . . no foot speed.": Tony Barnhart, *Always a Bulldog* (Chicago, Triumph Books, 2011), p. 304.
70 Patton thought Dooley . . . hard as he could.: Barnhart, *Always a Bulldog*, p. 309.

SOURCES

Arnzen, Chris. "Alec Millen." *Iron Sharpens Iron*. 19 Nov. 2008. sharpens. blogsports.com/2008/11/mp3-available-here_19.html.

Barnhart, Tony. *Always a Bulldog: Players, Coaches and Fans Share their Passion for Georgia Football*. Chicago: Triumph Books, 2011.

-----. *What It Means to Be a Bulldog: Vince Dooley, Mark Richt, and Georgia's Greatest Players*. Chicago; Triumph Books, 2004.

Bernarde, Scott. "UGA Equestrian Team Set to Defend National Title." *Atlanta Journal-Constitution*. 25 March 2010. http://www.ajc.com/sports/uga/uga-equestrian-team.

Bolton, Clyde. *The Crimson Tide: A Story of Alabama Football*. Huntsville, AL: The Strode Publishers, 1972.

-----. *War Eagle: A Story of Auburn Football*. Huntsville, AL: The Strode Publishers, 1973.

Branch, Jonathan. "Football Notebook: QB Murray Gets First Win." *DOGbytes online.com*. 27 Oct. 2012. http://www.dogbytesonline.com/football-notebook-qb-murray-gets-first-win.

Clarkson, Roger. "Big Man, Big Plans," *DOGBytesonline.com*, Oct. 19, 2012, http://www.dogbytesonline.com/big-man-big-plans.

-----. "Dogs' Gentle Giant," *DOGBytesonline.com*, Aug 9, 2011, http://www. dogbytesonline.com/dogs-gentle-giant-47490.

-----. "UGA's Earls on Road to Recovery." *OnlineAthens.com*. 4 July 2011. http://www.onlineathens.com/storeis/070411/gym_85236044.shtml.

Cromartie, Bill. *Clean Old-Fashioned Hate*. Huntsville, AL: The Strode Publishers, 1977. 34.

Dooley, Vince. *Dooley's Play Book: The 34 Most Memorable Plays in Georgia Football History*. Athens: Hill Street Press, 2008.

Dooley, Vince with Blake Giles. *Tales from the 1980 Georgia Bulldogs*. Champaign: IL, Sports Publishing L.L.C., 2005.

Dooley, Vince with Loran Smith. *Dooley's Dawgs: 40 Years of Championship Athletics at the University of Georgia*. Atlanta: Longstreet Press, 2003.

Echoes of Georgia Football: The Greatest Stories Ever Told. Ed. Ken Samelson. Chicago: Triumph Books, 2006.

Garbin, Patrick. *"Then Vince Said to Herschel . . .": The Best Georgia Bulldog Stories Ever Told*. Chicago: Triumph Books, 2007.

Higgins, Ron. "SEC Traditions: Pollack is Still a Showstopper." *SEC Digital Network*. 9 Dec. 2011. http://www.secdigitalnetwork.com/SECNation/SECTraditions/tabid/1073/Article/229991.

-----. "SEC Traditions: The Dooley Family Tree." *SEC Digital Network*. 2 Sept. 2010. http://www.secdigitalnetwork.com/SECNation/SECTraditions/tabid/1073/Article/134279.

-----. "SEC Traditions:Uga VIII." *SEC Digital Network*. 22 Oct. 22 2010. http://www.secdigitalnetowkr.com/SECNation/SECTraditions/tabid/1073/Article/21644.

"The History of the University of Georgia Redcoat Band 1905-2005,"http://www.bands.music/uga.edu/redcoat/history.php.

Hix, Tim. *Hoop Tales: Georgia Bulldog Men's Basketball*. Guilford, CN: The Globe Pequot Press, 2006.

-----. *Stadium Stories: Georgia Bulldogs*. Guilford, CN: The Globe Pequot Press, 2006.

Kendall, Josh. "Moreno, Teammates Mount Day-Long Georgia Celebration." *The Telegraph*. 28 Oct. 2007. 1C.

Kindred, Dave. "Germ Study a Model Role for Volleyball 'Gym Rat.'" *The Atlanta Journal/The Atlanta Constitution*. 21 Jan. 1996. E3.

Lidz, Franz. "Mirror, Mirror." *Sports Illustrated*. 15 Nov. 1999. http://www.sports illustrated.cnn.com/vault/article/magazine/MAG1017687/index.htm.

Magill, Dan. *Dan Magill's Bull-Doggerel: Fifty Years of Anecdotes from the Greatest Bulldog Ever*. Atlanta: Longstreet Press, 1993.

Outlar, Jesse. *Between the Hedges: A Story of Georgia Football*. Huntsville, AL: The Strode Publishers, 1974. 67.

Smith, Loran. *Wally's Boys*. Athens: Longstreet Press, 2005.

Smith, Loran with Lewis Grizzard. *Glory! Glory! Georgia's 1980 Championship Season: The Inside Story*. Atlanta: Peachtree Publishers Limited, 1981.

Starrs, Chris. "UGA Snapper Frix Has a Story to Tell." *DOGbytesonline.com*. 29 Dec. 2012. http://www.dogbytesonline.com/uga-snapper-frix-has-a-story-to-tell.

Stegeman, John F. *The Ghosts of Herty Field*. Athens: The University of Georgia Press, 1997.

Suggs, Rob. *Top Dawg: Mark Richt and the Revival of Georgia Football*. Nashville, Thomas Nelson, 2008.

Todd, Terry. "My Body's Like an Army," *Sports Illustrated*, Oct. 4, 1982, http://sportsillustrated.cnn.com/vault/article/magazine/MAG1125982/index.htm.

Towers, Chip. "Redemption." *OnlineAthens.com*. 17 Nov. 1996. http://www.onlineathens.com/1996/111796/1117.dogs.html.

Weizner, Marc. "Dogs Showed 'Mental, Physical Toughness in Win." *DOGbytes online.com*. 9 Sept. 2012. htttp://www.dogbytesonline.com/dogs-showed-mental-physical-toughness-in-win.

-----. "Missouri DT Gets in First Verbal Jabs." *DOGbytesonline.co*m. 3 Sept. 2012. http://www.dogbytesonline.com/mizzou-dt-gets-in-first-verbal-jabs.

-----. "Quick Hits: Dawson Yet to Meet with NCAA." *DOGbytesonline.com*. 5 Sept. 2012. http://www.dogbytesonline.com/quick-hits-dawson-yet-to-meet.

-----. "Welcome to the SEC." *DOGbytesonline.com*. Sept. 9, 2012. http://www.dogbytesonline.com/welcome-to-the-sec.

Wodraska, Lya. "No Skirting the Issue at UGA." *The Atlanta Journal/The Atlanta Constitution*. 20 Jan. 1993. F7.

Yoculan, Suzanne and Bill Donaldson. *Perfect 10: The University of Georgia Gymdogs and the Rise of Women's College Gymnastics in America*. Athens: Hill Street Press LLC, 2006.